★ WEAPONS OF WAR
MODERN FIGHTER AIRCRAFT
1945–PRESENT

★ WEAPONS OF WAR
MODERN FIGHTER AIRCRAFT
1945–PRESENT

CHARTWELL
BOOKS, INC.

CHARTWELL BOOKS, INC.
A division of BOOK SALES, INC.
276 Fifth Avenue Suite 206
New York, New York 10001
USA

© 2013 by Amber Books Ltd

Contributing authors: Chris Chant, Steve Crawford, Martin J. Dougherty, Ian Hogg,
Robert Jackson, Chris McNab, Michael Sharpe, Philip Trewhitt

ISBN 978-0-7858-2996-6

Printed in China

PICTURE CREDITS
Photographs:
Art-Tech/Aerospace: 7, 8/9
Dassault: 19
Luiz Perez: 6
Claude Rossi: 10 bottom
Saab Gripen: 18
U.S. Department of Defense: 11–17 all, 20–23 all
Claude Versiana: 10 top

All artworks © Art-Tech/Aerospace and Tom Cooper

CONTENTS

Introduction

Modern fighters

Jet fighters have come to dominate modern air warfare, usually in a multi-role capacity.

The first faltering steps into military jet technology were made some 70 years ago, in the golden era of canvas and wire aeroplanes and steam engines. As early as 1928, RAF Officer Frank (later Sir Frank) Whittle patented the design of an engine based on a theory of propulsion that was destined to revolutionize global transportation. It would have taken a brave man, however, among the privileged few who witnessed the first run of Frank Whittle's crude jet engine, or the first flight of the Heinkel He 178, to predict the enormous impact that the jet engine would have on

the aviation scene and on society as a whole. The effect has been nothing less than revolutionary. Jet propulsion has enabled aircraft to fly to new heights and ever greater speeds. Transcontinental travel has become commonplace. Indeed, it is often said that the world itself has become a 'smaller place'. All of this can be attributed to the jet engine and the men whose faith, vision and tenacity created it. Although they were divided by nationality, politics and even war, the jet pioneers are united by a common military affiliation. In the case of Frank Whittle, this proved as much of a hindrance

GLOSTER METEOR: see page 77

MIG-15: see page 116

as a benefit; for Ernst Heinkel, working in a country that prided itself on the practical application of technology, the opposite was true.

It would not be untrue to say that the single biggest motivating factor for the development of the jet engine was the desire to produce better, more capable and thus more lethal aircraft for military purposes. Whittle foresaw his engines powering transonic aircraft on transatlantic mail routes, but struggled with officialdom throughout the 1930s to generate anything approaching the enthusiasm his pioneering research merited. Only when the dark clouds of war hung over Europe was Whittle accorded the resources he needed. By 1941, Whittle was still struggling manfully with a small team that represented the entire Allied jet research programme. In Germany the jet propulsion programme had started later and yet had spawned the first jet aircraft. By comparison, in 1941 six separate teams – backed by substantial investment from the Third Reich – were employed in solving the inherent problems of the new technology.

WEAPONS OF WAR

AERMACCHI M.B.-326: see page 27

MIRAGE III: see page 57

TUCANO: see page 70

WEAPONS OF WAR

The first proper jet fighter was the Messerschmitt Me 262, employed by Nazi Germany from 1944.

When it became clear that Germany had stolen the lead in creating the first flying jet aircraft, it was perhaps inevitable that it would field the first jet aircraft in combat. In 1944, the Messerschmitt 262-A1 began operations and proved itself more than capable of catching the fastest and highest-flying aircraft the Allies could field. Suddenly the piston-engined aircraft was outmoded. The impact of the Me 262 on the air war over Europe was lessened to a degree by Hitler's insistence that many production aircraft should be equipped as fighter-bombers to attack advancing Allied forces (Me 262-1a), when they could have been far better employed in the interceptor role. Me 262 units were also forced to operate from

bases in Germany that were subject virtually to constant attack from advancing Allied forces. Had the Me 262 entered service a year earlier, the air war over Europe would almost certainly have proved less decisive.

The Allies had nothing in the league of the Me 262. The Gloster Meteor F. Mk 1 began operational service in July 1944, but a poor rate of climb and modest range made it unsuitable for combat. The British Air Ministry had generously supplied the US with complete access to British research into jet technology, enabling the Americans to consolidate the Allied effort and throw behind it the might of their aircraft industry, but nevertheless when World War II ended the Germans were still far ahead. Germany

MIG-21U: see page 120

F-4 PHANTOM: see page 103

WEAPONS OF WAR

F-5: see page 137

The victorious Allies stripped Germany of its jet expertise in the immediate post-war period.

was systematically stripped of her jet expertise by all the victorious powers, eager to lay their hands on this revolutionary new technology. Britain possessed similar expertise, but failed to exploit it, reduced her aircraft industry to a level of stagnation and thus lost the lead in jet technology. The influence of German research can be seen in the designs of American and Soviet aircraft for the next decade (the rocket that took men to the Moon has its ancestry in the V-2 rocket). Perhaps the most significant area of German research was in aerodynamics, particularly the swept wing. By incorporating this with jet propulsion, the gate was opened for a new generation of high-speed, supersonic aircraft.

MIG-15 VERSUS SABRE

If the summer of 1944 was the baptism of the military jet, then it earned its spurs in the Korean War. The United States Air Force (USAF) entered the war confident in the belief that it possessed the most advanced aircraft technology in the world, and the early actions of the war seemed to bear this fact out. Nothing prepared it for the profound shock of confronting Soviet-built MiG-15s in the skies over Korea. This agile, quick little fighter at once redressed

F-15 EAGLE: see page 111

The North American F-84 Sabre was developed in response to the appearance of the MiG-15.

the balance in air power over Korea and proved to the West that the Soviets had both the technology and industrial capacity to produce advanced jet aircraft. The appearance of the MiG-15 provoked a flurry of developments in the US. Foremost among these was the legendary North American F-84 Sabre. This aircraft, piloted by skilled and experienced pilots, did more than any other to win the air war in Korea. The war also highlighted some of the deficiencies of jet aircraft. Manoeuvrability had been

sacrificed for speed, take-off runs compared to piston-engined fighters were much longer (precluding jet operations from rough forward airstrips), and fuel consumption was prohibitively high for US squadrons forced to make long transit flights from southern bases to the combat area over the Yalu River.

During the early 1950s both the US and Soviet Union, with their overseas commitments, sought to develop more capable strategic attack aircraft to spearhead the so-called nuclear deterrent. The late

F-14D TOMCAT: see page 81

1950s was the heyday of the strategic bomber: large, multi-engined aircraft designed to deliver nuclear or conventional weapons to targets across thousands of miles of ocean. Both the United States and Soviet Union fielded jet bombers early in the 1950s, the Boeing B-52 Stratofortress and the Tupolev Tu-16 'Badger' among them. Britain, because of her strategic position in Europe, concentrated on defence but was the only other nation to develop a strategic bomber force, the famous V-bombers. These aircraft are some of the most enduring military jets ever built. The B-52, for example, is expected to serve well into the next century, albeit in a revised role as a missile platform.

THE DEVELOPMENT OF THE INTERCEPTOR

To counter the threat of the new generation of strategic jet bombers, both East and West were forced to re-evaluate the role of the interceptor. In response, a new generation of fast-climbing, radar-equipped aircraft were created that matched in complexity the bombers they were designed to destroy. A new word was coined to describe the complex package of electronic aids that the task demanded – avionics. Coupled with improving infrared and radar-guided missiles, these aircraft were the forerunners of today's air-superiority fighters. The English Electric Lightning, Convair Delta Dagger and Lockheed Starfighter were all borne out of the basic need to intercept enemy bombers, and served continuously in this role until the 1980s. To lessen the workload on the pilot, many interceptors were crewed by both a pilot and a radar/weapons officer.

F-16 FIGHTING FALCON: see page 75

SAAB JAS 39 GRIPEN: see page 153

More than a mention must be made of France during this period of military jet development. While its involvement in Korea was only limited, the French aviation industry recovered quickly after the war and, spearheaded by the energetic Marcel Dassault, became a major competitor in the military aircraft industry. French mistrust of US foreign policy precluded the purchase of US aircraft, and as a result France rapidly advanced into the jet age. Readers will observe the wide range and diversity of aircraft produced by French manufacturers during the 1950s and early 1960s. These aircraft have enabled the air forces of many smaller nations to enter the jet age sooner than they could have hoped if forced to rely on indigenous development. The US, Soviet Union, UK and France produced the vast majority of military jets during the 1950s and early 1960s, and aircraft produced by these countries were exported widely and supplied gratis to friendly nations. To reflect this fact, I have chosen some of the lesser known variants of aircraft such as the de Havilland Vampire and Hawker Sea Hawk,

WEAPONS OF WAR

RAFALE M: see page 60

or Dassault's enduring Mirage series in the plethora of national markings in which they have flown.

One of the most remarkable exceptions to the dominance of the four nations mentioned is Sweden. From the early 1950s this small, neutral nation developed some of the most advanced, cost-effective and capable military jet fighter aircraft ever built, independent of the support of any other nation. However, in general the military aviation industry was monopolized by the major powers. Investment by both superpowers into research and development reached enormous levels in the early 1960s, with experimental aircraft such as the North American B-70 Valkyrie swallowing up huge amounts of capital. When America entered the Vietnam War in 1965, her armed forces possessed the most advanced aircraft in the world, covering a wide range of roles from transport to aerial reconnaissance. A good indication of the rapid advances that had been made by the United States is to compare the Valkyrie with the Bell P-59A Airacomet, America's first jet aircraft produced barely 20 years previously.

Instances of air-to-air combat during the Vietnam War were few and far between. By far the greatest threat faced by American pilots were the surface-to-air missiles (SAMs) that many contemporary analysts believed would spell the end of the manned fighter aircraft. The US lost far more aircraft to Soviet-built SAMs than they did to North Vietnamese aircraft, and in response they rapidly developed dedicated electronic countermeasures (ECM) aircraft to counter the threat. The changing nature of air combat is perhaps best reflected in the long service of the F-4 Phantom II. Designed as a carrier-based fighter, it was developed into an attack aircraft, photo-reconnaissance aircraft, and finally as the F-4G 'Wild Weasel' ECM aircraft. Warfare again proved the greatest spur to military jet development, forcing the US to adapt its aircraft. For this conflict at least, though, the military jet played second fiddle to the most important aircraft available to US military commanders – the helicopter.

COMBAT EXPERIENCE

The late 1960s saw something of a lull in the arms race. This allowed the Soviet Union, which had previously relied on strength in numbers over technical sophistication with regard to its aircraft, to produce more advanced types. The MiG-23, 25 and 27 represented a significant advance in Soviet combat capability, matched by the Tupolev Tu-22 'Backfire' series that endures to this day. Exports of Soviet aircraft to the Middle East gave nations such as Egypt, Libya and Iraq greater combat capability, as demonstrated during the 1967 Six-Day War and again in the 1973 Arab-Israeli War. In the end this proved insufficient to defeat the technically superior Israeli Air Force, flying French and US-built aircraft, but it did give the Soviet Union valuable opportunities to evaluate its aircraft in combat. The late 1960s also heralded the arrival of a revolutionary new form of aircraft, the Vertical/Short TakeOff and Landing (V/STOL) Hawker Siddley Harrier, which to date has no real equal anywhere in the world.

Decreasing defence budgets and reduced order books forced many Western manufacturers to consolidate their efforts

F/A-18 HORNET: see page 112

MIG-29: see page 125

The end of the Cold War has changed strategic considerations and emphasised the need for rapidly deployable forces.

in the 1970s, the era that produced the majority of the current generation of military jet aircraft. Thus McDonnell teamed with Douglas and produced arguably the greatest fighter of the modern age, the F-15. In Europe, an alliance of Britain, Italy and Germany developed the Tornado, and will produce the next generation of aircraft to replace it. A number of new manufacturers have emerged onto the scene, with many smaller nations such as Taiwan, Japan, Argentina and South Africa keen to break

their reliance on imports and develop their indigenous aerospace industries. The end of the Cold War has changed strategic considerations and emphasized the need for rapidly deployable forces and multi-role combat aircraft to police international trouble spots. Stealth technology has emerged as the by-word of modern aviation, but as was demonstrated so forcefully during the 1991 Gulf War, the military jet continues to be the most potent and important symbol of military might.

F-22 RAPTOR: see page 96

Aeritalia G91T/1

The G91T variants were developed in the late 1950s to provide advanced flying and weapons training at transonic speeds. From the outset, it was intended to retain as much of the original G91 structure and equipment as possible. Externally, the aircraft can be distinguished by the two-seat cockpit, which necessitated extending the fuselage by 1.36m (4ft 5.5in). The aircraft could be rapidly converted to a combat role although avionics fit was slightly reduced; major users include Portugal and Germany, who took delivery of 66 of the T/3 models. The T/3 received updated flight equipment; 44 were built by Fiat (later amalgamated into Aeritalia) and 22 under licence by Dornier in Germany. Portugal was the last major user of the aircraft, which was replaced by the Aermacchi MB.339 after nearly 25 years' service in the Italian Air Force.

SPECIFICATIONS

COUNTRY OF ORIGIN: Italy
TYPE: twin-seat transonic trainer
POWERPLANT: one 2268kg (5000lb) Fiat-built Bristol Siddeley Orpheus 803 turbojet
PERFORMANCE: maximum level speed at 1520m (5000ft) 1030km/h (640mph); service ceiling 12,200m (40,000ft); operational radius (standard fuel) 320km (200 miles)
WEIGHT LOADED: basic operating weight 3865kg (8520lb); maximum takeoff weight 6050kg (13,340lb)
DIMENSIONS: wingspan 8.56m (28ft 1in); length overall 11.67m (38ft 4in); height overall 4.45m (14ft 7in); wing area 16.42m² (176.74ft²)
ARMAMENT: two 12.7mm (0.5in) machine guns; two underwing pylons for light bombs, missiles, or extra fuel tanks

Aeritalia G91T/3

The Fiat G91T/3 was a version of the T/1 produced for the Federal German Air Force. This aircraft was operated by Wattenschule 50. Keen to develop the G91 to its maximum possible potential, the Fiat designers proposed a new version of the T/1, known as the T/4. The reasoning behind this proposal was logical. In the early 1960s, the Italian Air Force had bought the European licence-built version of Lockheed's Starfighter, the F-104G. To provide some measure of flight training on this difficult aircraft the company proposed fitting the T/1 airframe with the electronics from the Starfighter. It was an ambitious project but technically a feasible one. Nevertheless, it never progressed beyond the project stage. Note the high visibility paint for maximum conspicuousness during training missions.

SPECIFICATIONS

COUNTRY OF ORIGIN: Italy
TYPE: twin-seat transonic trainer
POWERPLANT: one 2268kg (5000lb) Fiat-built Bristol Siddeley Orpheus 803 turbojet
PERFORMANCE: maximum level speed at 1520m (5000ft) 1030km/h (640mph); service ceiling 12,200m (40,000ft); operational radius (standard fuel) 320km (200 miles)
WEIGHT LOADED: basic operating weight 3865kg (8520lb); maximum takeoff weight 6050kg (13,340lb)
DIMENSIONS: wingspan 8.56m (28ft 1in); length overall 11.67m (38ft 4in); height overall 4.45m (14ft 7in); wing area 16.42m^2 (176.74ft^2)
ARMAMENT: two 12.7mm (0.5in) machine guns; two underwing pylons for light bombs, missiles, or extra fuel tanks

Aermacchi M-346

The M-346 is an advanced fighter trainer tailored to the new generation of fighters now coming into service. The project began in 1993 as a joint venture between Aermacchi and Yakolev, and the prototype first flew in 1996. Since then, development has proceeded separately, with the present M-346 being far more advanced than the original. This aircraft first flew in 2004 and incorporates avionics systems based on those of new-generation fighters. The M-346 has many performance characteristics in common with new fighters, such as the ability to manoeuvre at very high angles of attack. This enables pilots to train realistically without the costs associated with putting flight hours on a fighter airframe. The M-346 has nine hardpoints for weapons and, like many trainers, has a theoretical secondary light strike capability. It can also outperform many older fighters in air-to-air combat.

SPECIFICATIONS

COUNTRY OF ORIGIN: Italy
TYPE: two-seat jet trainer
POWERPLANT: two Honeywell F-124GA-200 delivering 2850kg (6,280lbf) thrust per engine
PERFORMANCE: maximum speed: 1083km/h (673mph) at 1524m (5000ft) ; initial climb: 6401m/min (21,000ft/min); ceiling: 13,716m (45,000ft); range: 1443km (903 miles)
WEIGHT LOADED: empty: 4610kg (10,165lb); maximum takeoff: 9500kg (20,944lb)
DIMENSIONS: span: 9.72m (31ft 11in); length: 11.49m (37ft 8in); height 4.98m (16ft 4in)
ARMAMENT: 3000kg (6614lb) of gun pods, rockets, bombs and missiles

Aermacchi M.B.326B

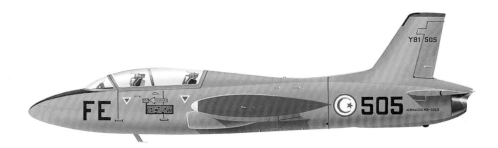

The 326B is one of the most important light attack and trainer aircraft to have emerged in the past four decades. The initial prototype flew in 1957; the basic airframe designed by Ermanno Bazzocchi of Aermacchi around a Rolls Royce Viper turbojet is conventional, with a well-equipped tandem cockpit ahead of a slightly swept leading edge low/mid wing monoplane. The Aeronautica Militare Italia received the first of 85 M.B.326s in February of 1962. Vice-free and predictable handling characteristics enabled the service to use the aircraft for all stages of flying training. In the training role, the M.B.326 has provided the AMI with a superb crossover trainer, which provided countless pilots with jet experience prior to moving on to faster jets. Tunisia purchased eight armed trainer M.B.326s in 1965, which are painted in high-visibility orange.

SPECIFICATIONS

COUNTRY OF ORIGIN: Italy
TYPE: two-seat basic/advanced trainer
POWERPLANT: one 1134kg (2500lb) Rolls Royce Viper 11 turbojet
PERFORMANCE: maximum speed 806km/h (501mph); standard range 1665km (1035 miles)
WEIGHT LOADED: empty 2237kg (4930lb) maximum take-off 3765kg (8300lb)
DIMENSIONS: span over tip tanks 10.56m (34ft 8in); length 10.65m (34ft 11in); height 3.72m (12ft 2in); wing area 19m^2 (204.5ft^2)
ARMAMENT: two optional 7.7mm (0.3in) machine guns, six underwing pylons with provision for machine gun pods, rockets and/or bombs, or camera pods, up to a maximum of 907kg (2000lb)

Aero L-29 Delfin

The Czech designed L-29 Delfin was selected in 1961 as the basic jet trainer of the Soviet Union in whose service the aircraft gained the NATO reporting name 'Maya'. Total production by Aero Vodochodny Narodni Podnik exceeded 3600. The L-29 is a simple, rugged aircraft that can be operated from grass, sand, or waterlogged airstrips. First entering service in 1963, the production lines remained in operation for the next 11 years. The Soviets took more than 2000 of the production total; deliveries were also made to almost every Communist Bloc air force. Many were exported to Soviet allies in the Middle East and Africa, where they are still in service. This aircraft wears the desert scheme of the Egyptian Air Force. The Egyptian aircraft can be configured for use in the attack role, and are fitted with equipment to suit.

SPECIFICATIONS

COUNTRY OF ORIGIN: Czechoslovakia
TYPE: two-seat basic and advanced trainer
POWERPLANT: one 890kg (1960lb) Motorlet M 701 VC-150 turbojet
PERFORMANCE: maximum speed at 5000m (16,400ft) 655km/h (407mph); service ceiling 11,000m (36,100ft); standard range 640km (397 miles)
WEIGHT LOADED: empty 2280kg (5027lb); maximum take-off 3280kg (7231lb)
DIMENSIONS: wingspan 10.29m (33ft 8in); length 10.81m (35ft 6in); height 3.13m (10ft 3in); wing area 19.80m² (213.1ft²)
ARMAMENT: none

Aero L-39C Albatros

First entering service in 1974 with the Czech air force, the L-39 succeeded the L-29 as the standard jet trainer for the air forces of Czechoslovakia, the Soviet Union and East Germany. The aircraft continues in this role today in the air forces of many former Eastern Bloc countries. The prototype L-39 first flew in November 1968 and it was obvious from the trials that vastly improved performance over the L-29 had been achieved. This was due mainly to the adoption of the Ivchyenko I-25 turbofan engine, which produced nearly double the power of the L-29's Motorlet unit. Throughout the design process, emphasis was placed on ease of maintenance. An auxiliary power unit allows the aircraft to operate independently of ground facilities. The L-39C is the basic trainer variant. Many have been sold on the private market, and are a common sight at aviation meets.

SPECIFICATIONS

COUNTRY OF ORIGIN: Czechoslovakia
TYPE: two-seat basic and advanced trainer
POWERPLANT: one 1720kg (3792lb) Ivchyenko AI-25TL turbofan
PERFORMANCE: maximum speed at 6000m (19,685ft) 780km/h (435mph); service ceiling 11,500m (37,730ft); standard range 1100km (683 miles)
WEIGHT LOADED: empty 3330kg (7341lb); maximum take-off 4700kg (10,632lb)
DIMENSIONS: wingspan 9.46m (31ft 1in); length 12.13m (39ft 10in); height 4.77m (15ft 8in); wing area 18.80m^2 (202.36ft^2)
ARMAMENT: none

Aérosp. (Fouga) CM.170 Magister

One of the most successful and widely used trainer aircraft in the world, the Magister was conceived and designed by Castello and Mauboussin for Fouga in 1950. It was the first purpose-built jet trainer in the world. Despite the unusual butterfly type tail, it proved a delight to fly. After prolonged testing, the Magister was put into production for the Armée de l'Air. Total production of this and the hooked navalised version (CM.75 Zephyr) was 437. Fouga was absorbed into the Potez company in 1958, which continued to produce a number of variants for international customers. In 1967, the Magister saw action during the Six-Day War with the Israeli Air Force. It was also previously the mount of the French national aerobatic team, the 'Patrouille de France'. The team now uses the Dassault/Dornier Alpha jet.

SPECIFICATIONS

COUNTRY OF ORIGIN: France
TYPE: two-seat trainer and light attack aircraft
POWERPLANT: two 400kg (882lb) Turbomeca Marbore IIA turbojets
PERFORMANCE: maximum speed at 9150m (30,000ft) 715km/h (444mph); service ceiling 11,000m (36,090ft); range 925km (575 miles)
WEIGHT LOADED: empty equipped 2150kg (4740lb); maximum takeoff 3200kg (7055lb)
DIMENSIONS: over tip tanks 12.12m (39ft 10in); length 10.06m (33ft); height 2.80m (9ft 2in); wing area 17.30m^2 (186.1ft^2)
ARMAMENT: two 7.5mm (0.295in) or 7.62mm (0.3in) machine guns; rockets, bombs or Nord AS.11 missiles on underwing pylons

AIDC Ching-Kuo IDF

The Ching-Kuo was developed in Taiwan to help that country overcome the considerable restrictions placed on foreign imports. The country had intended replacing its ageing fleet of F-104 Starfighters with the Northrop F-20 Tigershark, but this proved impossible when the US government placed an embargo on this and any other comparable advanced fighter. American expertise was therefore bought in from General Dynamics, Garrett, Westinghouse, Bendix/King and Lear who helped to finalise a design in 1985. The first prototype flew on 28 May 1989; from the outset, it was obvious that the production aircraft would bear many design characteristics familiar to the F-16 and F-18. The first aircraft was delivered to the Chinese Nationalist Air Force in 1994, although sales of the F-16 Fighting Falcon to Taiwan in 1992 reduced its production to a mere 130 aircraft.

SPECIFICATIONS

COUNTRY OF ORIGIN: Taiwan
TYPE: lightweight air-defence fighter with anti-ship capability
POWERPLANT: two 4291kg (9460lb) ITEC (Garrett/AIDC) TFE1042-70 turbofans
PERFORMANCE: maximum speed at 10,975m (36,000ft) 1275km/h (792mph); service ceiling 16,760m (55,000ft)
WEIGHT LOADED: normal take-off weight 9072kg (20,000lb)
DIMENSIONS: wingspan 9m (29ft 6in) over missile rails; length 14.48m (47ft 6in)
ARMAMENT: one 20mm (0.79in) General Electric M61A1 Vulcan rotary six-barrel cannon, six external pylons with provision for four Tien Chien 1 short range air-to-air missiles, or two Tien Chien 2 medium range air-to-air missiles, or four Tien Chien 1 and two Tien Chien 2, or three Hsiung Feng II anti-ship missiles and two Tien Chien 1 AAMs, or AGMs, or various combinations of rocket or cannon pods

Atlas Cheetah

Bearing a strong resemblance to the Israeli Kfir, the Atlas Cheetah is in fact the South African answer to an international arms embargo imposed on the country in 1977, which prevented the SAAF from importing a replacement for its ageing fleet of Mirage IIIs. The programme involved replacing nearly 50 percent of the airframe, and adding a host of improved features. Externally, a number of aerodynamic changes were made to the original airframe, the most obvious of which are the small inlet mounted canard foreplanes. The first aircraft was modified from a two-seat Mirage IIID2; production aircraft are modified from both single-seaters and twin-seaters, the twin-seaters possessing more advanced systems; all variants are configured to carry a host of indigenously produced weapons.

SPECIFICATIONS

COUNTRY OF ORIGIN: South Africa
TYPE: one/two-seat combat and training aircraft
POWERPLANT: one 7200kg (15,873lb) SNECMA Atar 9K-50 turbojet
PERFORMANCE: maximum speed above 12,000m (39,370ft) 2337km/h (1452mph); service ceiling 17,000m (55,775ft)
WEIGHT LOADED: not revealed
DIMENSIONS: wingspan 8.22m (26ft 12in); length 15.40m (50ft 6.5in); height 4.25m (13ft 12in); wing area 35m^2 (376.75ft^2)
ARMAMENT: two 30mm (1.18in) DEFA cannon, Armscor V3B and V3C Kukri air-to-air missiles, provision for external stores such as cluster bombs, laser designator pods, and rockets

Avro Canada CF-105 Arrow

The story of the Arrow bears a startling similarity to that of the BAC TSR.2. Both projects showed great promise during the early stages of development in the mid-1950s, and both were destroyed by the misguided decisions of politicians who were convinced that the days of the manned interceptor were numbered. The first stages of development of the Arrow, a two-seat all-weather interceptor, began in 1953, with planned entry into service as a replacement for the same company's CF-100 a decade later. Production of the first five prototypes began in April 1954. The design incorporated a huge high-set delta wing. The first flight of the aircraft was made on 25 March 1958, but a little under 10 months later, the whole project was cancelled. All the prototypes were destroyed in what must rank as one of the most short-sighted decisions made by any Canadian government.

SPECIFICATIONS

COUNTRY OF ORIGIN: Canada
TYPE: two-seat all-weather long range supersonic interceptor
POWERPLANT: two 10,659kg (23,500lb) Pratt and Whitney J75-P-3 turbojets
PERFORMANCE: Mach 2.3 recorded during tests
WEIGHT LOADED: empty 22,244kg (49,040lb); average take-off during trials 25,855kg (57,000lb)
DIMENSIONS: wingspan 15.24m (50ft); length 23.72m (77ft 10in); height 6.48m (21ft 3in); wing area 113.8m^2 (1225ft^2)
ARMAMENT: eight Sparrow air-to-air missiles in internal bay

BAC (EE) Lightning F.Mk 1A

W.E.W. 'Teddy' Petter was again the driving force behind the aircraft that was for a period during the 1960s the most formidable interceptor in the world. The Lightning developed from a prototype built by English Electric, called the P.1, which first flew in August 1954. The P.1 was powered by two Bristol Siddeley Sapphire engines mounted 'under and over', and fed by a common inlet. P.1B was a completely redesigned version to meet the British government Specification F.23/49, with a two-shock intake. With Avon engines fitted, Mach 2 was attained in November 1958. Twenty pre-production aircraft were built before the first F.Mk 1 entered service in 1960. The F.Mk 1A had provision for flight refuelling and UHF radio. The Lightning was a complicated aircraft for its time, and maintenance time per flying hour was high.

SPECIFICATIONS

COUNTRY OF ORIGIN: United Kingdom
TYPE: single-seat all-weather interceptor
POWERPLANT: two 6545kg (14,430lb) Rolls Royce Avon turbojets
PERFORMANCE: maximum speed at 10.970m (36,000ft) 2414km/h (1500mph); service ceiling 18,920m (60,000ft); range 1440km (895 miles)
WEIGHT LOADED: empty 12,700kg (28,000lb); maximum take-off 22,680kg (50,000lb)
DIMENSIONS: wingspan 10.61m (34ft 10in); length 16.84 m (55ft 3in); height 5.97m (19ft 7in); wing area 35.31m² (380.1ft²)
ARMAMENT: interchangeable packs of two all-attitude Red Top or stern chase Firestreak air-to-air missiles or two 30mm (1.18in) Aden guns, in forward part of belly tank

BAC (EE) Lightning F.Mk 6

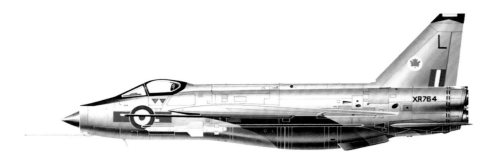

The last single-seat fighter aircraft to see service with the Royal Air Force entered service in 1960. The history of the aircraft can be traced back to 1947, when the RAF issued a study contract to the English Electric company for a supersonic research aircraft, the P.1B. After nearly ten years of development work, during which time the company was amalgamated into the British Aircraft Corporation, the first Lightning F.1s were delivered. In service the aircraft proved to be as good as any all-weather interceptor then available, with a phenomenal top speed and rate of climb. However, it was hampered by poor duration. On the recommendation of BAC the RAF decided to modify the much improved F.3 to F.6 standard in 1965. The F.6 featured and extensively modified ventral tank and a cambered, kinked wing leading edge, to allow operations at greater weights.

SPECIFICATIONS

COUNTRY OF ORIGIN: United Kingdom
TYPE: supersonic all-weather interceptor, strike and reconnaissance aircraft
POWERPLANT: two 7112kg (15,680lb) Rolls Royce Avon 302 afterburning turbojets
PERFORMANCE: maximum speed 2415km/h (1500mph, Mach 2.3) at 12,190m (40,000ft); standard range 1287km (800 miles); initial rate of climb 15,240m (50,000ft) per minute
WEIGHT LOADED: empty equipped 12,700kg (28,000lb); maximum take-off 22,680kg (50,000lb)
DIMENSIONS: wingspan 10.61m (34ft 10in); length 16.84 m (55ft 3in); height 5.97m (19ft 7in); wing area 35.31m^2 (380.1ft^2)
ARMAMENT: two 30mm (1.18in) Aden guns in ventral pack (120 rounds), two Fire Streak or Red Top air-to-air missiles, or five Vinten 360 70mm (2.76in) cameras, or night reconnaissance cameras and linescan equipment and underwing flares; underwing/overwing pylons for up to 144 rockets or six 454kg (1000lb) bombs missiles, or five Vinten 360 70mm (2.76in) cameras, or night reconnaissance cameras and linescan equipment and underwing flares; underwing/overwing pylons for up to 144 rockets or six 454kg (1000lb) bombs

BAe (HS) Hawk T.Mk 1

The Hawk has been one of the truly outstanding successes of the British aerospace industry in the past three decades. Much of this success is due to the exceptional service life of the airframe, low maintenance requirements (the lowest per flight hour of any jet aircraft in the world), relatively inexpensive purchase price when originally offered for export, large optional payload, and its ability to operate in the medium range attack and air superiority role for a fraction of the cost of more powerful types. The Hawk was the only entirely new all-British military aircraft for 15 years in 1980. The first prototype flew in August 1974, and the first two operational aircraft were handed over in November 1976. Construction of the efficient Adour turbofan is modular, enabling easy maintenance. The basic RAF advanced trainer is designated the T.Mk 1.

SPECIFICATIONS

COUNTRY OF ORIGIN: United Kingdom
TYPE: two-seat basic and advanced jet trainer
POWERPLANT: one 2359kg (5200lb) Rolls Royce/Turbomeca Adour Mk 151 turbofan
PERFORMANCE: maximum speed 1038km/h (645mph); service ceiling 15,240m (50,000ft); endurance 4 hours
WEIGHT LOADED: empty 3647kg (8040lb); maximum take-off 7750kg (17,085lb)
DIMENSIONS: wingspan 9.39m (30ft 10in); length 11.17m (36ft 8in); height 3.99m (13ft 1in); wing area 16.69m² (179.64ft²)
ARMAMENT: underfuselage/wing hardpoints with provision for up to 2567kg (5660lb) of stores

BAe (HS) Hawk T.Mk 1A

As well as its fleet of T.Mk 1 trainer aircraft the RAF also operates the aircraft for weapons instruction. Nos 1 and 2 Tactical Weapons Units, previously based at RAF Brawdy and RAF Chivenor, have now been incorporated into the Flying training school at RAF Valley. The T.Mk1A has three pylons; the central one is normally occupied by a 30mm (1.18in) Aden cannon, the two underwing pylons can be fitted with a wide combination of weapons, including Matra rocket pods. The Hawk has in various formats been exported to more than 14 different countries, often as a dedicated attack aircraft. In 1985 construction began of the Hawk Mk 200, a single-seat version dedicated to the tactical attack role. This aircraft served with No.1 Tactical Weapons Unit at Brawdy in Wales and is carrying a centreline drop tank and rocket pods for weapons training.

SPECIFICATIONS

COUNTRY OF ORIGIN: United Kingdom
TYPE: two-seat weapons training aircraft
POWERPLANT: one 2359kg (5200lb) Rolls Royce/ Turbomeca Adour Mk 151 turbofan
PERFORMANCE: maximum speed 1038km/h (645mph); service ceiling 15,240m (50,000ft); endurance 4 hours
WEIGHT LOADED: empty 3647kg (8040lb); maximum take-off 7750kg (17,085lb)
DIMENSIONS: wingspan 9.39m (30ft 10in); length 11.17m (36ft 9in); height 3.99m (13ft 1in); wing area 16.69m^2 (179.64ft^2)
ARMAMENT: underfuselage/wing hardpoints with provision for up to 2567kg (5660lb) of stores, wingtip mounted air-to-air missiles

BAe Sea Harrier FRS.Mk 1

The Sea Harrier FRS.Mk 1 was ordered to equip the three Royal Navy 'throughdeck cruisers' (a strange name dreamed up by defence staff for the Invincible class carriers) in fighter, anti-submarine and surface-attack roles, with Blue Fox radar and other weapons. Official policy during the time of the land-based Harrier's gestation was that all future Royal Navy combat aircraft must be helicopters, and this delayed development of its carrier borne equivalent until 1975. Installing the Blue Fox radar meant lengthening the nose, and the cockpit was raised to accommodate a more substantial avionics suite and to afford the pilot a better all-round view. Introduced into service shortly before the Falklands War, the aircraft proved an incalculably important asset during that conflict. The aircraft has pictured three of its Argentine victims stencilled on its nose.

SPECIFICATIONS

COUNTRY OF ORIGIN: United Kingdom
TYPE: shipborne multi-role combat aircraft
POWERPLANT: one 9752kg (21,500lb) Rolls-Royce Pegasus Mk.104 vectored thrust turbofan
PERFORMANCE: maximum speed at sea level 1110km/h (690mph) with maximum AAM load; service ceiling 15,545m (51,000ft); intercept radius 740km (460 miles) on high level mission with full combat reserve
WEIGHT LOADED: empty 5942kg (13,100lb); maximum take-off 11,884kg (26,200lb)
DIMENSIONS: wingspan 7.7m (25ft 3in); length 14.5m (47ft 7in); height 3.71m (12ft 2in); wing area 18.68m^2 (201.1ft^2)
ARMAMENT: two 30mm Aden cannon with 150 rounds, five external pylons with provision for AIM-9 Sidewinder or Matra Magic air-to-air missiles, and two Harpoon or Sea Eagle anti-shipping missiles, up to a total of 3629kg (8000lb)

BAe Sea Harrier FRS.Mk 2

In 1985, on orders from the Ministry of Defence and the Fleet Air Arm, British Aerospace began the development of an upgrade programme to modernise the fleet of FRS. Mk 1s. The primary aim of the program was to give the Sea Harrier the ability to engage multiple beyond-visual-range targets with the new AIM-120 AMRAAM medium-range air-to-air missile. The most obvious difference is to the shape of the forward fuselage, which accommodates the new Ferranti Blue Vixen pulse-Doppler track-while-scan radar. Further upgrades to the avionics include a MIL 1553B digital databus, redesigned HUD and dual head-down displays, Marconi Sky Guardian Radar Warning Receiver, and a secure data and voice link system. Two additional missile launch rails and the new Aden 25 cannon complete the package. Deliveries of the 33 converted aircraft commenced in April 1992.

SPECIFICATIONS

COUNTRY OF ORIGIN: United Kingdom
TYPE: shipborne multi-role combat aircraft
POWERPLANT: one 9752kg (21,500lb) Rolls-Royce Pegasus Mk 106 vectored-thrust turbofan
PERFORMANCE: maximum speed at sea level 1185km/h (736mph) at sea level with maximum AAM load; service ceiling 15,545m (51,000ft); intercept radius 185km (115 miles) on hi-hi-hi CAP with 90 minuted loiter on station
WEIGHT LOADED: empty 5942kg (13,100lb); maximum take-off 11,884kg (26,200lb)
DIMENSIONS: wingspan 7.7m (25ft 3in); length 14.17m (46ft 6in); height 3.71m (12ft 2in); wing area 18.68m^2 (201.1ft^2)
ARMAMENT: two 25mm (1in) Aden cannon with 150 rounds, five external pylons with provision for AIM-9 Sidewinder, AIM-120 AMRAAM, and two Harpoon or Sea Eagle anti-shipping missiles, up to a total of 3629kg (8000lb)

BAe/M. Douglas T-45A Goshawk

The Goshawk is a development of the highly successful BAe (HS) Hawk trainer for the US Navy. A joint McDonnell Douglas/BAe venture based Hawk emerged as the winner of a competition announced by the US Navy in the late 1970s for a carrier-equipped naval pilot trainer to replace the Rockwell T-2 Buckeye. The aircraft is significantly different from the Hawk, with strong twin-wheel nose gear, strengthened long-stroke main gear legs, an arrestor hook, and twin lateral airbrakes. Other changes include US Navy-style cockpit and avionics, and US Navy standard avionics. Emphasis was placed on the need for operational economy, and the Rolls-Royce/Turbomeca engine has been designed with this in mind. The aircraft, which are built by McDonnell in Missouri, entered service in 1990. Pictured is a T-45A Goshawk of Training Wing Two at Kingsville, Texas.

SPECIFICATIONS

COUNTRY OF ORIGIN: United States
TYPE: tandem-seat carrier-equipped naval pilot trainer
POWERPLANT: one 2651kg (5845lb) Rolls Royce/Turbomeca F-405-RR-401 turbofan
PERFORMANCE: maximum speed at 2440m (8000ft) 997km/h (620mph); service ceiling 12,875m (42,250ft); range on internal fuel 1850km (1150 miles)
WEIGHT LOADED: empty 4263kg (9399lb); maximum take-off 5787kg (12,758lb)
DIMENSIONS: wingspan 9.39m (30ft 10in); length 11.97m (39ft 3in); height 4.27m (14ft); wing area 16.69m² (179.6ft²)
ARMAMENT: none

Bell P-59A Airacomet

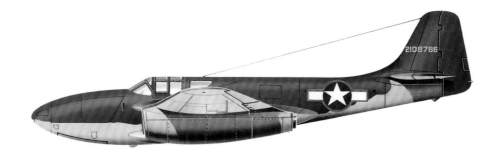

Development work on jet aircraft began rather later in America than in Europe, and with the considerable assistance of British expertise. In June 1941 the US government and General 'Hap' Arnold of the US Army Air Corps were told of Britain's development of the turbojet engine. On 5 September, 1941 Bell Aircraft was requested to design a jet fighter and in October a Whittle turbojet. Complete engineering drawings and a team from Power Jets Ltd (Whittle's private company) arrived from Britain to hasten proceedings. Barely a year later, the Bell P-59A Airacomet was ready to fly, with Whittle engines built by General Electric. Development went extremely well, and 12 YP-59As were delivered for service trials in 1944. The P-59A was classed as a fighter trainer when it became clear that it would not make an effective front-line fighter. Total procurement amounted to 66.

SPECIFICATIONS

COUNTRY OF ORIGIN: United States
TYPE: single-seat jet fighter trainer
POWERPLANT: two (907kg) 2,000lb General Electric J31-GE-3
PERFORMANCE: maximum speed 671km/h (413mph); service ceiling 14,080m (46,200ft); maximum range with two 125 Imp gal drop tanks 837km (520 miles)
WEIGHT LOADED: empty 3610kg (7950lb); maximum take-off 6214kg (13,700lb)
DIMENSIONS: wingspan 13.87m (45ft 6in); length 11.63m (38ft 11in); height 3.66m (12ft); wing area 35.84m^2 (385.8ft^2)
ARMAMENT: none

Boeing F/A-18E/F Super Hornet

The F/A-18 Super Hornet was developed from the F/A-18 Hornet, which first flew in 1978. The E model is a single-seat version, with the two-seater designated F/A-18F. The Hornet was created as a relatively inexpensive fighter and attack platform, but suffered from a very short combat range using internal fuel. The Super Hornet is more than a new version; it is larger and was significantly redesigned to incorporate lessons learned since the introduction of its predecessor. The Super Hornet is able to carry a range of weapons, switching from air defence to strike or anti-ship roles quickly. It can also function as a tanker with the addition of external fuel tanks and a buddy-refuelling system. Operationally, Hornets have proven very robust and survivable aircraft, and are expected to serve until the F-35 is available in sufficiently numbers.

SPECIFICATIONS

COUNTRY OF ORIGIN: United States
TYPE: single- or two-seat twin-engined multirole combat aircraft
POWERPLANT: one General Electric F-414-GE-400 delivering 98kN (22,000lb) thrust per engine
PERFORMANCE: maximum speed: 1915km/h (1197mph); initial climb classified; ceiling 18,288m (60,000ft); range 1443km (903 miles)
WEIGHT LOADED: empty 13,387kg (29,574lbs); maximum takeoff: 29,937kg (66,000lbs)
DIMENSIONS: wingspan 13.62m (44ft 9in); length 18.31m (60ft 1in); height 4.88m (16ft)
ARMAMENT: one M61A1 20mm (0.79in) Vulcan cannon; 8050kg (17,750lbs) of additional stores

Canadair CF-5 Freedom Fighter

When the Canadian government selected the Northrop F-5 for its air force, Canadair Ltd in Montreal was chosen to built the aircraft under licence in two versions, the CF-5A single-seat version and the CF-5D tandem seat aircraft. Canadair were able to incorporate a number of significant improvements to the design; the most important upgrade being uprated engines than the original US model. The potential range of the aircraft was also improved by fitting an inflight refuelling probe. Canadair have successfully exported the aircraft to a number of countries, including the Netherlands. In 1987 Bristol Aerospace received a contract to update 56 CF-5A/Ds for further use as lead-in trainers by the Canadian Air Force. This programme extended airframe life by 4000 hours and, with other improvements, should allow the aircraft to remain in service well into the next century.

SPECIFICATIONS

COUNTRY OF ORIGIN: United States and Canada
TYPE: fighter and light attack aircraft
POWERPLANT: two 1950kg (4300lb) Orenda (General Electric) J85-CAN-15 turbojets
PERFORMANCE: maximum speed at 10,970m (36,000ft) 1575km/h (978mph); service ceiling 15,500m (50,580ft); combat radius at maximum load 314km (195 miles)
WEIGHT LOADED: empty 3700kg (8157lb); maximum take-off 9249kg (20,390lb)
DIMENSIONS: wingspan 7.87m (25ft 10in); length 14.38m (47ft 2in); height 4.01m (13ft 2in); wing area 15.79m^2 (170ft^2)
ARMAMENT: two 20mm (0.79in) M39 cannon, underwing hardpoints with provision for two AIM-9 Sidewinder AAMs, gun and rocket pods, and bombs

Canadair CL-41G-5 Tebuan

The Tebuan has been the standard jet trainer of the Canadian Armed forces for over 30 years. In service the aircraft is known by the designation CT-114. The aircraft represented a significant step for the Canadian aerospace industry, as it was the first aircraft designed and built solely in that country. Early development was privately funded by the company because of a lack of interest from the Canadian government. Two prototypes were built powered by the built Pratt & Whitney JT12-A5 turbojet. Production examples were fitted with the indigenously built version of the General Electric CJ610, made in Canada as the J85-CAN-40. Production orders totalled some 190 aircraft, with 20 extensively modified CL-41G-5 Tebuan aircraft for Malaysia. The majority of the Canadian aircraft are based with No. 2 Flying Training Scholl at Moose Jaw in Saskatchewan.

SPECIFICATIONS

COUNTRY OF ORIGIN: Canada
TYPE: two-seat jet trainer
POWERPLANT: one 1338kg (2950lb) Orenda (General Electric) J85-CAN-40 turbojet
PERFORMANCE: maximum speed 797km/h (495mph); service ceiling 13,100m (43,000ft); standard range 1000km (621 miles)
WEIGHT LOADED: empty 2220kg (4895lb); maximum take-off 3532kg (7787lb)
DIMENSIONS: wingspan 11.13m (36ft 6in); length 9.75m (32ft); height 2.76m (9ft 1in); wing area 20.44m^2 (220ft^2)
ARMAMENT: six external hardpoints with provision for up to 1814kg (4000lb) of stores

Canadair Sabre Mk 4

Italy was one of nearly 20 countries which operated the North-American designed Sabre. Fiat licence-built 221 of the F-86K version for the Aeronautica Militare Italia. This aircraft, however, is a Sabre Mk 4 (F-86E), one of 430 built by the Canadair company with funds provided by the Mutual Defense Assistance Program to re-equip RAF fighter squadrons. The aircraft were later fitted with extended leading edges and passed on to Italy, who took 180, Yugoslavia, Greece and Turkey. Unlike the Canadair-built Sabres Mk 5 and Mk 6, which were powered by a licence-built Orenda turbojet, the Mk 4 aircraft had the original General Electric engine. In all other respects the Mk 4 was the same as the F-86E, including the 'all-flying tail'. Note the prancing horse insignia on the tail, reminiscent of the badge used on a certain marque of Italian car.

SPECIFICATIONS

COUNTRY OF ORIGIN: United States and Canada
TYPE: single-seat fighter-bomber
POWERPLANT: one 2358kg (5200lb) General Electric J47-GE-13 turbojet
PERFORMANCE: maximum speed at sea level 1091km/h (678mph); service ceiling 15,240m (50,000ft); range 1344km (835 miles)
WEIGHT LOADED: empty 5045kg (11,125lb); maximum loaded 9350kg (20,611lb)
DIMENSIONS: wingspan 11.30m (37ft 1in); length 11.43m (37ft 6in); height 4.47m (14ft 9in); wing area 27.76m^2 (288ft^2)
ARMAMENT: six 12.7mm (0.5in) Colt-Browning M-3 with 267rpg, underwing hardpoints for two tanks or two stores of 454kg (1000lb), plus eight rockets

Canadair Sabre Mk 6

Canadair continued their association with the Sabre through the Mk 5 (370 built) and the Mk 6 (655 built). The Mk 5 introduced a feature that was already in production by North American; the 6-3 leading edge, which extended the wing root leading edge by 15cm (6in) and the tip leading edge by 7.6cm (3in). This modification improved agility in high-speed combat. The South African Air Force, who flew F-86E and F aircraft with UN forces in the Korean War, purchased 34 of the Mk 6 version, with a 3300kg (7275lb) Orenda engine. This aircraft is widely regarded as the finest dogfighter of the era, and remained in use with the SAAF until replaced by the Mirage F1CZ and F1AZ in the 1970s. The aircraft pictured served with No. 1 Squadron. Commonwealth Aircraft Corporation in Australia were also involved in Sabre production.

SPECIFICATIONS

COUNTRY OF ORIGIN: United States and Canada
TYPE: single-seat fighter-bomber
POWERPLANT: one 3300kg (7275lb) Orenda 14 turbojet
PERFORMANCE: maximum speed at sea level 1091km/h (678mph); service ceiling 15,240m (50,000ft); range 1344km (835 miles)
WEIGHT LOADED: empty 5045kg (11,125lb); maximum loaded 9350kg (20,611lb)
DIMENSIONS: wingspan 11.30m (37ft 1in); length 11.43m (37ft 6in); height 4.47m (14ft 9in); wing area 27.76m^2 (288ft^2)
ARMAMENT: six 12.7mm (0.5in) Colt-Browning M-3 with 267rpg, underwing hardpoints for two tanks or two stores of 454kg (1000lb), plus eight rockets

CASA C-101EB-01 Aviojet

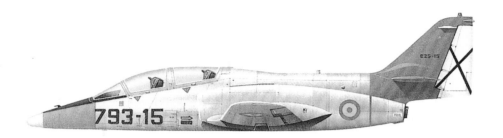

The C-101 was developed by the Spanish CASA company (Construcciones Aeronauticas SA) from the mid-1970s as a replacement for Hispano HA.200 jet trainer in service with the Spanish Air Force (EdA). Assistance in the design was provided by Northrop and MBB, and many of the parts were sourced from foreign contractors, including the Dowty-built landing gear, Martin-Baker ejector seats, Garrett-AiResearch turbofan and Sperry flight control system. The first flight was made in June 1977. Production deliveries of the 92 aircraft supplied to the EdA began in 1980. From 1990 CASA upgraded the weapons system on the C-101 in the hope of encouraging export orders. These were forthcoming from Honduras (four C-101BB), Chile (for a licence-built version designated T-36 and the upgraded C-101CC, which are designated A-36) and Jordan, who operate the C-101CC aircraft.

SPECIFICATIONS

COUNTRY OF ORIGIN: Spain
TYPE: two-seat advanced flying/weapons trainer
POWERPLANT: one 1588kg (3500lb) Garrett AiResearch TFE731-2-2J turbofan
PERFORMANCE: maximum speed at 6095m (20,000ft) 806km/h (501mph); service ceiling 12,800m (42,000ft); endurance 7 hours
WEIGHT LOADED: empty 3470kg (7650lb); maximum take-off 4850kg (10,692lb)
DIMENSIONS: wingspan 10.6m (34ft 9in); length 12.5m (41ft); height 4.25m (13ft 11in); wing area 20m² (215.3ft²)
ARMAMENT: one 30mm (1.18in) DEFA cannon; six external hardpoints with provision for up to 2000kg (4410lb) of stores, including rocket pods, missiles, bombs and drop tanks

Chance Vought F7U-1 Cutlass

The Cutlass was designed in 1946, when fighter aerodynamics had been thrown into considerable turmoil by wartime German research and emerging jet technology. The design incorporated a 38-degree swept wing carrying wide-span powered elevons, airbrakes, and full-span leading edge slats. Twin vertical tails were mounted at one-third span. These features were remarkably advanced for the time, as was the use of afterburning engines, an automatic stabilization system, and controls with artificial feedback. Three prototype XF7U-1s were completed, and the first of these flew on 29 September 1949. After only 14 F7U-1s had been completed, the production run was halted and a number of major design revisions were made. Even so, the F7U-2 suffered severe engine difficulties and the final productions version, the F7U-3 and missile-armed 3-M, had non-afterburning engines.

SPECIFICATIONS

COUNTRY OF ORIGIN: United States
TYPE: carrier-based fighter-bomber
POWERPLANT: two 1905kg (4200lb) Westinghouse J34-32 turbojets
PERFORMANCE: maximum speed at sea level 1070km/h (665mph); service ceiling 12,500m (41,000ft); combat radius with maximum fuel 966km (600 miles)
WEIGHT LOADED: empty 5385kg (11,870lb); maximum take-off 7640kg (16,840lb)
DIMENSIONS: wingspan 11.78m (38ft 8in); length 12.07m (39ft 7in); height 3m (9ft 10in); wing area 46.08m² (496ft²)
ARMAMENT: four 20mm (0.79in) M-2 cannon

Convair F-102 Delta Dagger

In 1948 Convair flew the world's first delta wing aircraft, the XF-92A, which was part of a program intended to lead to a supersonic fighter. This was terminated, but the US Air Force later issued a specification for an extremely advanced allweather interceptor to carry the Hughes MX-1179 electronic control system. This effectively made the carrier aircraft subordinate to its avionics, a radical concept in the early 1950s. The contract was contested between six airframe manufacturers, and awarded to Convair in September 1961. In the event the Hughes ECS system could not be delivered in time and was rescheduled for the F-106 program. Early flight trials of the F-102 prototype were disappointing, but once the design was right right, 875 were delivered. In the search mode the pilot flew with two control columns; the left hand being used to adjust the sweep angle and range of the radar.

SPECIFICATIONS

COUNTRY OF ORIGIN: United States

TYPE: supersonic all-weather single-seat fighter-interceptor

POWERPLANT: one 7802kg (17,200lb) Pratt & Whitney J57-P-23 turbojet

PERFORMANCE: maximum speed at 10,970m (36,000ft) 1328km/h (825mph); service ceiling 16,460m (54,000ft); range 2172km (1350 miles)

WEIGHT LOADED: empty 8630kg (19,050lb); maximum take-off 14,288kg (31,500lb)

DIMENSIONS: wingspan 11.62m (38ft 2in); length 20.84m (68ft 5in); height 6.46m (21ft 3in); wing area 61.45m² (661.5ft²)

ARMAMENT: two AIM-26/26A Falcon missiles, or one AIM-26/26A plus two AIM-4A Falcons, or one AIM-26/26A plus two AIM-4C/Ds, or six AIM-4As, or six AIM-4C/Ds, some aircraft fitted with 12 70mm (2.75in) folding-fin rockets

Convair F-106 Delta Dart

The F-106 was originally designated F-102B to indicate the strong family connection with the earlier Delta Dagger. The aircraft is notable because of the fact that it was designed from the outset as an integral weapon system, in which each of the differing units (airframe, weapons, etc.) would integrate as a compatible system. Central to this project was an electronic weapons control system. It had been hoped to realise this objective with the Delta Dagger, but delays in the program meant that the ECS was not ready until late in 1955, an unacceptable time scale to the USAF who planned to bring the F-102 into service that year. The F-106 program was delayed by engine problems, and flight tests proved disappointing. The Hughes designed MA-1 ECS was also not performing well. The aircraft eventually entered service in October 1959 and remained in service, in updated versions, until 1988.

SPECIFICATIONS

COUNTRY OF ORIGIN: United States
TYPE: light attack and reconnaissance aircraft
POWERPLANT: two 1293kg (2850lb) General Electric J85-GE-17A turbojets
PERFORMANCE: maximum speed at 4875m (16,000ft) 816km/h (507mph); service ceiling 12,730m (41,765ft); range with 1860kg (4100lb) load 740km (460 miles)
WEIGHT LOADED: empty 2817kg (6211lb); maximum take-off 6350kg (14,000lb)
DIMENSIONS: wingspan including tip tanks 10.93m (35ft 10in); length 8.62m (29ft 3in); height 2.7m (8ft 10in); wing area 17.09m^2 (183.9ft^2)
ARMAMENT: one 7.62mm (0.3in) GAU-2 Minigun six-barrelled machine gun, eight underwing hardpoints with provision for more than 2268kg (5000lb) of stores, including bombs, rocket and gun pods, napalm tanks, and other equipment

Dassault M.D. 450 Ouragan

The Second World War effectively destroyed the French aircraft industry, and it had to be largely rebuilt from scratch while learning the new technology of jet propulsion. Most companies in the newly nationalized French aviation industry failed to see any of their designs built in any quantity, but the private firm of Dassault produced what is undoubtedly one of the most enduring and successful families of combat aircraft in the world. The whole line of Mirages, Etendards, Mystères, and Rafales stem from the simple, conventional, but highly effective Ouragan (Hurricane) of 1949. Powered by a licence built version of the British Rolls-Royce Nene turbojet, the first unarmed prototype was flown on 28 February 1949. Equipped with a pressurized cockpit and wingtip fuel tanks, the first of 150 production aircraft entered service in 1952.

SPECIFICATIONS

COUNTRY OF ORIGIN: France
TYPE: single-seat fighter/ground attack aircraft
POWERPLANT: one 2300kg (5070lb) Hispano-Suiza Nene 104B turbojet
PERFORMANCE: maximum speed 940km/h (584mph); service ceiling 15,000m (49,210ft); range 1000km (620 miles)
WEIGHT LOADED: empty 4150kg (9150lb); maximum take-off 7600kg (17,416lb)
DIMENSIONS: wingspan over tip tanks 13.2m (43ft 2in); length 10.74m (35ft 3in); height 4.15m (13ft 7in); wing area 23.8m^2 (256.18ft^2)
ARMAMENT: four 20mm (0.79in) Hispano 404 cannon; underwing hardpoints for two 434kg (1000lb) bombs, or 16 105mm (4.13in) rockets, or eight rockets and two 458 litre (101 gal) napalm tanks

Dassault Mirage 2000B

Because of the complexity of the third generation Mirage 2000, the French air force decided to pursue a programme of development for a two-seat trainer to run concurrently with the single-seat 2000C. The fifth Mirage 2000 prototype was flown in this format as the 2000B in October 1980. Production aircraft are distinguished by a slightly longer (7.5in) fuselage, and are not fitted with internal cannon. Internal fuel capacity is also reduced from 3980 to 3870 litres (1051 to 1022 gal). The 2000B retains full operational capability in French service and first flew on 7 October 1983. Escadron de Chasse 1/2 'Cigognes' was the first French air force unit to become operational at Dijon on 2 July 1984. This aircraft has the famous 'stork' emblem of EC1/2 'Cigognes'. The aircraft has also been ordered by at least five countries in various formats to complement their single-seat fleets.

SPECIFICATIONS

COUNTRY OF ORIGIN: France
TYPE: dual-seat jet trainer with operational capability
POWERPLANT: one 9700kg (21,834lb) SNECMA M53-P2 turbofan
PERFORMANCE: maximum speed at high altitude 2338km/h (1453mph); service ceiling 18,000m (59,055ft); range with two 1700 litre (374 gal) drop tanks 1850km (1150miles)
WEIGHT LOADED: empty 7600kg (16,755lb); maximum take-off 17,000kg (37,480lb)
DIMENSIONS: wingspan 9.13m (29ft 11in); length 14.55m (47ft 9in); height 5.15m (16ft 11in); wing area 41m² (441.3ft²)
ARMAMENT: seven external pylons with provision for R.530 air-to-air missiles, AS.30 or A.30L missiles, rocket launcher pods, and various attack loads including 454kg (1000lb) bombs. For air defence weapon training the Cubic Corporation AIS (airborne instrumentation subsystem) pod, which resembles a Magic missile, may be carried

Dassault Mirage 2000C

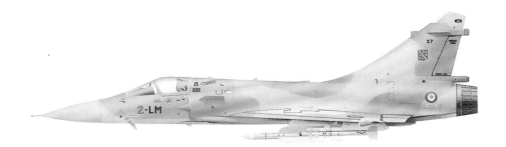

Early research and experience
had shown that the delta wing
configuration carried some notable
disadvantages, not least a lack of
low speed manoeuvrability. With the
development of fly-by-wire technology
during the late 1960s and early 1970s,
it was possible for airframe designers to
overcome some of these problems, when
coupled with advances in aerodynamics.
The 2000C was designed by Dassault to
be a single-seat interceptor to replace
the F1. The aircraft was adopted by the
French government in December 1975 as
the primary combat aircraft of the French
air force, and was developed initially
under contract as an interceptor and
air superiority fighter. Deliveries to the
Armée de l'Air began in July 1984; early
production examples were fitted with the
SNEMCA M53-5; aircraft built after that
date have the more powerful M53-P2.

SPECIFICATIONS
COUNTRY OF ORIGIN: France
TYPE: single-seat air-superiority and attack fighter
POWERPLANT: one 9700kg (21,834lb) SNECMA
M53-P2 turbofan
PERFORMANCE: maximum speed at high altitude
2338km/h (1453mph); service ceiling 18,000m
(59,055ft); range with 1000kg (2205lb) load 1480km
(920 miles)
WEIGHT LOADED: empty 7500kg (16,534lb);
maximum take-off 17,000kg (37,480lb)
DIMENSIONS: wingspan 9.13m (29ft 11in); length
14.36m (47ft 1in); height 5.20m (17ft 1in); wing
area 41m^2 (441.3ft^2)
ARMAMENT: two DEFA 554 cannon with 125rpg;
nine external pylons with provision for up to 6300kg
(13,889lb) of stores, including R.530 air-to-air
missiles, AS.30 or A.30L missiles, rocket launcher
pods, and various attack loads including 454kg
(1000lb) bombs. For air defence weapon training
the Cubic Corpn AIS (airborne instrumentation
subsystem) pod, which resembles a Magic missile,
may be carried

Dassault Mirage 2000H

In 1998 Dassault completed its contract to deliver 136 Mirage 2000C aircraft to the Armée de l'Air. Export contracts for the agile and capable 2000C have been justifiably plentiful; by 1990 the French company had received firm orders from Abu Dhabi, Egypt, Greece, India and Peru. The Indian aircraft pictured is one of 40 ordered in October 1982 which carry the designation 2000H. Final delivery was made in September 1984. The first of two Indian squadrons was formed at Gwalior AB on 29 June 1985, when the 2000H received the Indian name Vajra, meaning 'Thunder'. A follow-on order was signed in March 1986 for a further nine aircraft (six H and three TH). This aircraft is operated by No. 225 Squadron of the Indian Air Force and is pictured with drop tanks fitted. A two-seat low-level strike version is offered as the Mirage 2000N.

SPECIFICATIONS

COUNTRY OF ORIGIN: France
TYPE: single-seat air-superiority and attack fighter
POWERPLANT: one 9700kg (21,834lb) SNECMA M53-P2 turbofan
PERFORMANCE: maximum speed at high altitude 2338km/h (1453mph); service ceiling 18,000m (59,055ft); range with 1000kg (2205lb) load 1480km (920 miles)
WEIGHT LOADED: empty 7500kg (16,534lb); maximum take-off 17,000kg (37,480lb)
DIMENSIONS: wingspan 9.13m (29ft 11in); length 14.36m (47ft 1in); height 5.20m (17ft 1in); wing area 41m² (441.3ft²)
ARMAMENT: two DEFA 554 cannon with 125rpg; nine external pylons with provision for up to 6300kg (13,889lb) of stores, including R.530 air-to-air missiles, AS.30 or A.30L missiles, rocket launcher pods, and various attack loads including 454kg (1000lb) bombs. For air defence weapon training the Cubic Corpn AIS (airborne instrumentation subsystem) pod may be carried

Dassault Mirage F1CK

The F1 once again demonstrates the willingness of the Dassault company to risk privately funded ventures. Recognising that the Mirage III family would eventually become redundant, the French government awarded Dassault a development contract for a successor, dubbed the F2. The aircraft was large with a conventional swept wing, breaking away from the classic Mirage form. Dassault privately funded a smaller version of the F2, called the F1, which was sized to be powered by a single Atar engine. The Armée de l'Air subsequently chose to purchase this model. The aircraft marked a huge advance on the tailless delta form of previous models, with lower landing speeds and take-off runs. Other advances were made in the avionics suite and integral tankage for 45 percent more fuel. Manoeuvrability was also substantially improved. Pictured is the F1CK, in service in Kuwait.

SPECIFICATIONS

COUNTRY OF ORIGIN: France
TYPE: single-seat multi-mission fighter attack aircraft
POWERPLANT: one 7200kg (15,873lb) SNECMA Atar 9K-50 turbojet
PERFORMANCE: maximum speed at high altitude 2350km/h (1460mph); service ceiling 20,000m (65,615ft); range with maximum load 900km (560 miles)
WEIGHT LOADED: empty 7400kg (16,314lb); maximum take-off 15,200kg (33,510lb)
DIMENSIONS: wingspan 8.4m (27ft 7in); length 15m (49ft 2in); height 4.5m (14ft 9in); wing area 25m² (269.11ft²)
ARMAMENT: two 30mm (1.18in) 553 DEFA cannon with 135rpg, five external pylons with provision for up to 6300kg (13,889lb) of stores; Magic air-to-air missiles on wingtip rails, weapons include Matra Super 530 air-to-air missiles, conventional and laser guided bombs, rockets, AS.30L laser-guided air-to-surface missiles, AM.39 Exocet anti-ship missiles, ARMAT anti-radiation missiles, or Durandal, Belouga, or BAP anti-runway weapons

Dassault Mirage F1EQ5

Iraq's changing political allegiances since Saddam Hussein assumed control of the country are reflected in the widely varying aircraft types operated by the Iraqi Air Force. This was well demonstrated during the 1980 Iran/Iraq and 1991 Gulf wars. During the first conflict, France was the major supplier of Iraqi aircraft, having delivered no less than 89 Mirage F1s. Included in this order was a batch of 29 F1EQ5s with Agave radar for over-water operations and armed with Exocet antishipping missiles. These aircraft were delivered in October 1984 after much delay, and became operational in February the following year. At least 12 aircraft were equipped with SLAR (Sideways Looking Airborne Radar) and ground-data links for reconnaissance missions, alongside their normal fighter/bomber role. These aircraft operate alongside Soviet types, and were also used during the Gulf War.

SPECIFICATIONS

COUNTRY OF ORIGIN: France

TYPE: single-seat multi-mission fighter attack aircraft

POWERPLANT: one 7200kg (15,873lb) SNECMA Atar 9K-50 turbojet

PERFORMANCE: maximum speed at high altitude 2350km/h (1460mph); service ceiling 20,000m (65,615ft); range with maximum load 900km (560 miles)

WEIGHT LOADED: empty 7400kg (16,314lb); maximum take-off 15,200kg (33,510lb)

DIMENSIONS: wingspan 9.32m (30ft 7in); length 15.3m (50ft 3in); height 4.5m (14ft 9in); wing area 25m^2 (269.11ft^2)

ARMAMENT: two 30mm (1.18in) 553 DEFA cannon with 135 rpg, five external pylons with provision for up to 6300kg (13,889lb) of stores; Magic air-to-air missiles on wingtip rails, weapons include Matra Super 530 air-to-air missiles, conventional and laser guided bombs, rockets, AS.30L laser-guided air-to-surface missiles, AM.39 Exocet anti-ship missiles, ARMAT antiradiation missiles, or Durandal, Belouga, or BAP anti-runway weapons

Dassault Mirage IIIEA

The hugely successful Mirage program has brought incalculable prestige to the French aviation industry in the past four decades. The early prototype aircraft was conceived to meet an Armée de l'Air light interceptor specification of 1952. Once again Dassault found the powerplant insufficient and produced a larger, heavier, and more powerful aircraft, the Mirage III. On 24 October 1958 pre-production Mirage IIIA-01 became the first West European fighter to attain Mach 2 in level flight. The production version was designated the IIIC, a slightly developed version with either guns or a booster rocket for faster climb. Altogether 244 models were delivered to the Armée de l'Air, South Africa, and Israel. From this model emerged the longer and heavier IIIE for ground attack, with the Atar 9C turbojet and increased internal fuel. This variant first appeared on 20 April 1961.

SPECIFICATIONS

COUNTRY OF ORIGIN: France
TYPE: single-seat day visual fighter bomber
POWERPLANT: one 6200kg (13,668lb) SNECMA Atar 9C turbojet
PERFORMANCE: maximum speed at sea level 1390km/h (883mph); service ceiling 17,000m (55,755ft); combat radius at low level with 907kg (2000lb) load 1200km (745 miles)
WEIGHT LOADED: empty 7050kg (15,540lb); loaded 13,500kg (27,760lb)
DIMENSIONS: wingspan 8.22m (26ft 11in); length 16.5m (56ft); height 4.50m (14ft 9in); wing area 35m^2 (376.7ft^2)
ARMAMENT: two 30mm (1.18in) DEFA 552A cannon with 125rpg; three external pylons with provision for up to 3000kg (6612lb) of stores, including bombs, rockets and gun pods

Dassault Mystère IIC

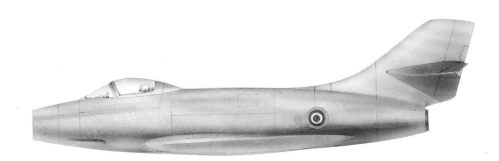

Marcel Dassault's design philosophy was always to progress in easy steps. The first Mystère was merely an M.D. 450 Ouragan with 30 degrees of sweep to the wings and tail. This aircraft, designated the Mystère I, first flew in February 1951. Over the course of the following two years, eight further prototypes were built and flown. The original aircraft was powered by the ubiquitous Rolls-Royce Nene, while the remainder were fitted with a licence-built (by Hispano Suiza) version of the Tay. Pre-production aircraft were fitted with the all-French Atar axial engine, the first use of any French gas turbine for military aircraft propulsion. In April 1953, the Armee de l'Air ordered 150 of the fighters; ultimately 180 were built, 156 for France and 24 for Israel (never delivered). Service career was short, but the aircraft is important as the first swept-wing fighter to go into production in Europe.

SPECIFICATIONS

COUNTRY OF ORIGIN: France
TYPE: single-seat fighter bomber
POWERPLANT: one 3000kg (6600lb) SNECMA Atar 101D3 turbojet
PERFORMANCE: maximum speed 1060km/h (658mph); service ceiling 13,000m (42,650ft); range 1200km (745 miles)
WEIGHT LOADED: empty 5250kg (11,514lb); loaded 7450kg (16,442lb)
DIMENSIONS: wingspan 13.1m (42ft 11in); length 11.7m (38ft 6in); height 4.25m (13ft 11in)
ARMAMENT: two 30mm (1.18in) Hispano 603 cannon with 150 rounds each

Dassault Mystère IVA

Although superficially similar to the II series aircraft, the IVA was in fact a completely new aircraft, with hardly a single structural part being common to both. The wing of the IV was thinner, more sharply swept, and much strengthened. The fuselage and tail were completely new and the pilot enjoyed powered controls. The US Air Force tested the prototype, which first flew as M.D. 454-01 on 28 September 1952, and placed an off-shore contract for 225 of the production aircraft in April 1953. The first 50 production aircraft had the Rolls Royce Tay engine, but the remainder each had a Hispano Suiza Verdon 350. Exports orders were won from Israel and India, in addition to the aircraft supplied to the Armée de l'Air. The French aircraft saw action during the Suez conflict in 1956; several variants have been built with radar and with a dual cockpit.

SPECIFICATIONS

COUNTRY OF ORIGIN: France
TYPE: single-seat fighter bomber
POWERPLANT: one 2850kg (6280lb) Hispano Suiza Tay 250A turbojet; or 3500kg (7716lb) Hispano Suiza Verdon 350 turbojet
PERFORMANCE: maximum speed 1120km/h (696mph); service ceiling 13,750m (45,000ft); range 1320km (820 miles)
WEIGHT LOADED: empty 5875kg (11,514lb); loaded 9500kg (20,950lb)
DIMENSIONS: wingspan 11.1m (36ft 5in); length 12.9m (42ft 2in); height 4.4m (14ft 5in)
ARMAMENT: two 30mm (1.18in) DEFA 551 cannon with 150 rounds, four underwing hardpoints with provision for up to 907kg (2000lb) of stores, including tanks, rockets, or bombs

Dassault Rafale M

The Rafale has been designed and built to replace the Armée de l'Air's fleet of SEPECAT Jaguars, and to form part of the new French nuclear carrier force's air wing. Although both services considered the Eurofighter, they have opted instead for the Rafale, which is smaller and lighter than the multi-national aircraft. The Dassault company embarked on the project in early 1983, and the first flight took place on 4 July 1986. The airframe is largely constructed of composite materials, with a fly-by-wire control system. Early flight trials were particularly encouraging, with the aircraft achieving Mach 1.8 on only its second flight. Original production orders have been cut since the end of the Cold War. The three versions are the Rafale C single-seat operational aircraft for the Armée de l'Air, the Rafale B two seat multi-role aircraft, and the Rafale M navalized fighter (pictured).

SPECIFICATIONS

COUNTRY OF ORIGIN: France
TYPE: carrier based multi-role combat aircraft
POWERPLANT: two 7450kg (16,424lb) SNECMA M88-2 turbofans
PERFORMANCE: maximum speed at high altitude 2130km/h (1324mph); combat radius air-to-air mission 1853km (1152 miles)
WEIGHT LOADED: empty equipped 9800kg (maximum take-off 19,500kg (42,990lb)
DIMENSIONS: wingspan 10.90m (35ft 9in); length 15.30m (50ft 2in); height 5.34m (17ft 6in); wing area 46m² (495.1ft²)
ARMAMENT: one 30mm (1.18in) DEFA 791B cannon, 14 external hardpoints with provision for up to 6000kg (13,228lb) of stores, including air-to-air missiles, air-to-surface missiles, anti-ship missiles, guided and conventional bombs, rocket launchers, recce, Elint and jammer pods

Dassault Super Mystère B2

The Super Mystère developed from a Rolls Royce Avon-engined version of the Mystère IV, known as the IVB. The Mystère IVB was a major leap forward, with tapered, milled and che-milled sheets, integral tanks, flush aerials and a radar gunsight in the new nose. This aircraft proved to be a stepping stone to the bigger, heavier, and more powerful SMB.2, which introduced yet another new wing with 45 degrees of sweep and aerodynamics copied from the North American F-100 Super Sabre. The flattened nose also had more than a passing relationship to the American fighter. Although the first SMB.2 flew with the Rolls Royce Avon RA.7R, production examples were fitted with the Atar 101G. On its fourth flight, SMB.2-01, with Avon, easily exceeded Mach 1 in level flight, to make this the first supersonic aircraft to go into production, or in service.

SPECIFICATIONS

COUNTRY OF ORIGIN: France
TYPE: single-seat fighter bomber
POWERPLANT: one 4460kg (9833lb) SNECMA Atar 101 G-2/-3 turbojet
PERFORMANCE: maximum speed at 12,000m (39,370ft) 1195km/h (743mph); service ceiling 17,000m (55,775ft); range 870km (540 miles)
WEIGHT LOADED: empty 6932kg (15,282lb); maximum take-off 10,000kg (22,046lb)
DIMENSIONS: wingspan 10.52m (34ft 6in); length 14.13m (46ft 4in); height 4.55m (14ft 11in); wing area 35m^2 (376.75ft^2)
ARMAMENT: two 30mm DEFA 551cannon, internal Matra launcher for 35 SNEB 68mm rockets, two underwing hardpoints with provision for up to 907kg (2000lb) of stores, including tanks, rockets or bombs

D

Dassault/Dornier Alpha Jet E

There are two basic forms of the Alpha Jet, the attack version previously discussed, and the two seat jet trainer initially produced for the Armee de l'Air. Physically very similar to the attack version, the E (Ecole) replaced the Fouga Magister and Dassault Mystère as the basic and advanced jet trainers of the French Air Force. For all aircraft, the outer wings, tail unit, rear fuselage, landing gear doors and exhaust are manufactured in Germany; the forward and centre fuselage were manufactured in France, with other work contracted out to Belgian. The Alpha Jet made its first flight, at Istres, on 26 October 1973. A further development of the Ecole is Alpha Jet 3, fitted with state of the art cockpit controls and multiple cockpit displays for use in training aircrew with the navigation/attack systems of future aircraft.

SPECIFICATIONS

COUNTRY OF ORIGIN: France and Germany
TYPE: two-seat basic/advanced trainer aircraft
POWERPLANT: two 1350kg (2976lb) Turbomeca Larzac 04 turbofans
PERFORMANCE: maximum speed 927km/h (576mph); service ceiling 14,000m (45,930ft); low level training mission 540km (335 miles)
WEIGHT LOADED: empty 3345kg (7374lb); normal take-off 5000kg (11,023lb)
DIMENSIONS: wingpsan 9.11m (29ft 11in); length 11.75m (38ft 7in); height 4.19m (13ft 9in); wing area 17.5m^2 (188.37ft^2)
ARMAMENT: none

De Havilland Sea Vixen FAW Mk 2

The Sea Vixen, like many of the aircraft operated by the Royal Navy, was originally designed to a Royal Air Force requirement for a land-based all weather interceptor, first issued in 1946. The aircraft lost the competition to the Gloster Javelin. Fortunately for de Havilland, the Royal Navy had a similar requirement for a carrier based aircraft, and, after successful trials from the deck of HMS *Albion*, an initial order was placed in January 1955. The first 92 aircraft to be completed by the de Havilland factory at Christchurch were designated FAW. Mk 1s and featured a hinged and pointed radome, powerfolding wings and hydraulically steerable nosewheel. The later FAW Mk 2 had increased fuel capacity and provision for four Red Top missiles in place of the Firestreaks carried by the Mk 1. Most were brought up to Mk 2 standard by 1964 and remained in service until 1971.

SPECIFICATIONS

COUNTRY OF ORIGIN: United Kingdom
TYPE: two-seat all-weather strike fighter
POWERPLANT: two 5094kg (11,230lb) Rolls-Royce Avon 208 turbojets
PERFORMANCE: maximum speed 1110km/h (690mph) at 20,000ft at sea level; climb to 3050m (10,000ft) in 1 min 30 secs; service ceiling 21,790m (48,000ft); range about 600 miles (FAW 1) and 800 miles (FAW 2)
WEIGHT LOADED: empty weight about 22,000lb; maximum take-off 18,858kg (41,575lb)
DIMENSIONS: wingspan 15.54m (51ft); length 17.02 m (55ft 7in); height 3.28 m (10ft 9in); wing area 60.20m² (648ft²)
ARMAMENT: on four inboard wing pylons; four Firestreak air-to-air missiles (FAW 1) or four Red Top air-to-air missiles (FAW 2); on outer pylons 454kg (1000lb) bombs, Bullpup air-to-surface missiles or equivalent stores; as built, but not used, provision for 28 folding fin aircraft rockets in two flip-out boxes beneath cockpit floor

De Havilland Vampire FB.Mk 6

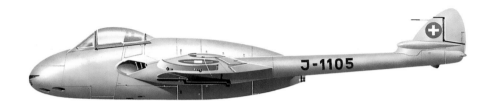

Production of an improved fighter-bomber version of the Vampire began in 1948 with the FB.Mk 5. This aircraft featured a restressed wing clipped from 12.19m to 11.58m (40ft to 38ft), with wing pylons capable of carrying either two 227kg (500lb) bombs or eight rocket projectiles. The FB.Mk 6 was the result of efforts to improve the performance of the Vampire, with an uprated version of the Goblin turbojet that afforded a marked increase in maximum speed. The FB.Mk 6 was not ordered by the RAF, but attracted much attention from overseas customers. At the time Switzerland was seeking a low-cost replacement for its fleet of Messerschmitt Bf 109s. The low cost and impressive performance of the Vampire persuaded the Swiss government to purchase 75 FB.Mk 6s. A licence was later granted to build the aircraft, and 100 were subsequently completed for the Swiss air force.

SPECIFICATIONS

COUNTRY OF ORIGIN: United Kingdom and Switzerland
TYPE: single-seat fighter bomber
POWERPLANT: one 1498kg (3300lb) de Havilland Goblin 35 turbojet
PERFORMANCE: maximum speed 883km/h (548mph); service ceiling 13,410m (44,000ft); range with drop tanks 2253km (1400 miles)
WEIGHT LOADED: empty 3266kg (7200lb); loaded with drop tanks 5600kg (12,290lb)
DIMENSIONS: wingspan 11.6m (38ft); length 9.37m (30ft 9in); height 2.69m (8ft 10in); wing area 24.32m^2 (262ft^2)
ARMAMENT: four 20mm (0.79in) Hispano cannon with 150 rounds, wing pylons capable of carrying either two 227kg (500lb) bombs or 27kg (60lb) rockets

De Havilland Vampire NF.Mk 10

The RAF was remarkably slow to order jet night-fighters, and the de Havilland company took the initiative to develop the D.H.113 NF.Mk 10 as a private venture. The aircraft was designed as a two-seater, and development was greatly speeded by the fact that the Vampire nacelle was similar in width to the nose of the Mosquito, so the crew compartment, AI Mk 10 radar and equipment of the NF versions could be transferred with the minimum of changes. Batches were delivered to the Egyptian air force before exports of arms to that country were banned in 1950. The RAF took over the contract and received 95 aircraft, which were first used by No 25 Squadron from West Malling in late 1951. The pilot and observer/radar operator sat close together in ordinary (non-ejecting) seats, which made emergency escape particularly hazardous.

SPECIFICATIONS

COUNTRY OF ORIGIN: United Kingdom
TYPE: two-seat night fighter
POWERPLANT: one 1520kg (3350lb) de Havilland Goblin turbojet
PERFORMANCE: maximum speed 885km/h (549mph); service ceiling 12,200m (40,000ft); range 1255km (780 miles)
WEIGHT LOADED: empty 3172kg (6984lb); loaded 5148kg (11,350lb)
DIMENSIONS: wingspan 11.6m (38ft); length 10.55m (34ft 7in); height 2m (6ft 7in); wing area 24.32m^2 (262ft^2)
ARMAMENT: four 20mm (0.79in) Hispano cannon

De Havilland Vampire T.Mk 11

The success of the two-seat night-fighter version of the Vampire logically led Airspeed Ltd (a de Havilland subsidiary) to embark on the development of a trainer as a private venture. The nose radar was removed and full dual flight controls were added to the pressurized, if somewhat cramped cockpit, to produce the D.H. 115 Vampire T.Mk 11. The prototype was first flown in November 1950, and service deliveries began to the AFS at Weston Zoyland and Valley in early 1952. In 1956, the T.Mk 11 became the standard jet trainer of the Royal Air Force, and at one time was the most numerous of its aircraft, with over 530 delivered. The production run totalled 731, with export deliveries (as T.Mk 55s) to 19 countries. Fifteen of the aircraft were still in service with the Swiss air force in 1990, although they have now been withdrawn.

SPECIFICATIONS

COUNTRY OF ORIGIN: United Kingdom
TYPE two-seat basic trainer
POWERPLANT: one 1589kg (3500lb) de Havilland Goblin 35 turbojet
PERFORMANCE: maximum speed 885km/h (549mph); service ceiling 12,200m (40,000ft); range on internal fuel 1370km (853 miles)
WEIGHT LOADED: empty 3347kg (7380lb); loaded (clean) 5060kg (11,150lb)
DIMENSIONS: wingspan 11.6m (38ft); length 10.55m (34ft 7in); height 1.86m (6ft 2in); wing area 24.32m² (262ft²)
ARMAMENT: two 20mm (0.79in) Hispano cannon

De Havilland Venom NF.Mk 2A

The two-seat radar-equipped night fighter version of the Venom was originally developed as a private venture, and flown without the equipment for combat use. Early flight trials during 1950 indicated that it handled well, although hampered by a poor rate of roll. Like the two-seat Vampire there was no provision for emergency escape (a fact that proved less than popular with aircrew) but in 1952 the type began production at Chester. The NF.Mk 2 differed from the FB.Mk 1 in having a widened fuselage to accommodate pilot and observer, and an extended nose for the radar equipment. The Mk 2A was a redesignation of the Mk 2 following incorporation of a clear view canopy and modifications made to the tail unit. A version of the Mk 2 supplied to the Royal Swedish Air Force was designated as the NF.Mk 51. Total production for the Mk 2 was 60.

SPECIFICATIONS

COUNTRY OF ORIGIN: United Kingdom
TYPE two-seat night fighter
POWERPLANT: one 2245kg (4950lb) de Havilland Ghost 104 turbojet
PERFORMANCE: maximum speed 1013km/h (630mph); service ceiling 15,000m (49,200ft); range 1610km (1000 miles)
WEIGHT LOADED: empty 4000kg (8800lb); loaded 7166kg (15,800lb)
DIMENSIONS: wingspan 12.70m (41ft 8in); length 11.17m (36ft 8in); height 1.98m (6ft 6in); wing area 24.32m² (262ft²)
ARMAMENT: four 20mm (0.79in) Hispano cannon

Douglas F4D-1 Skyray

Details of German research into delta wings generated great interest in the US Navy, prompting senior officers to request a design submission from Douglas based on the theories. This was finalised as a variation on a pure delta wing configuration in 1948, and Douglas were awarded a contract to build two prototypes in December of that year. The first aircraft made its maiden flight in January 1951 with an Allison turbojet, although continual engine problems during the development programme led to the selection of a Pratt & Whitney unit for production aircraft. The design was a cantilever mid-wing monoplane controlled by trailing edge elevons serving collectively as elevators or differentially as ailerons. The cockpit was situated well forward of the wing and afforded the pilot excellent all-round visibility.

SPECIFICATIONS

COUNTRY OF ORIGIN: United States
TYPE: single-seat carrier-based fighter
POWERPLANT: one 4626kg (10,200lb) Pratt & Whitney J57-P-8A turbojet
PERFORMANCE: maximum speed at 10,975m (36,000ft) 1162km/h (695mph); service ceiling above 16,765m (55,000ft); range 1931km (1200 miles)
WEIGHT LOADED: empty 7268kg (16,024lb); maximum take-off 11,340kg (25,000lb)
DIMENSIONS: wingspan 10.21m (33ft 6in); length 13.93m (45ft 8in); height 3.96m (13ft); wing area 51.75m^2 (557.03ft^2)
ARMAMENT: four 20mm (0.79in) cannon; six underwing hardpoints with provision for up to 1814kg (4000lb) of stores, including AIM-9C Sidewinder air-to-air missiles, bombs, rockets, or drop tanks

Eurofighter EF-2000 Typhoon

The agreement to develop the Eurofighter was signed in May 1988 between the UK, West Germany, and Italy. Spain joined in November of that year. The aircraft was designed ostensibly for the air-to-air role, with secondary air-to-surface capability. With the canard design and fly by wire control system it is hoped the aircraft will be supremely manoeuvrable in the air. Other advanced features include extensive use of composite materials for airframe construction and an advanced sensor and avionics suite. Flight testing is well underway, but the program has been consistently delayed by political and financial wrangling. The first aircraft should enter production in 2005. However, the Eurofighter is entering a highly competitive market, and with a unit price of £60 million plus, export orders may be hard won.

SPECIFICATIONS

COUNTRY OF ORIGIN: Germany, Italy, Spain, and United Kingdom
TYPE: multi-role fighter
POWERPLANT: two 9185kg (20,250lb) Eurojet EJ200 turbofans
PERFORMANCE: maximum speed at 11,000m (36,090ft) 2125km/h (1321mph); combat radius about 463 and 556km
WEIGHT LOADED: empty 9750kg (21,495lb); maximum take-off 21,000kg (46,297lb)
DIMENSIONS: wingspan 10.50m (34ft 5in); length 14.50m (47ft 4in); height 4.0m (13ft 2in); wing area 52.4m^2 (564.05ft^2)
ARMAMENT: one 27mm (1.06in) Mauser cannon; thirteen fuselage hardpoints for a wide variety of stores including ASRAAM, FMRAAM missile programs; also air-to-surface missiles, anti-radar missiles, guided and unguided bombs

Embraer Tucano

The widely exported Tucano first flew in 1980 and began delivery in 1983. Around 600 aircraft have been sold since then, mainly in small numbers for use as trainers. The Tucano has been used by numerous nations including Iraq, Peru, France, Argentina and its native Brazil. An upgraded licensed version, the Short Tucano, was built for the Royal Air Force. Another upgraded version was a contender for the US primary trainer role, but was not successful. In addition to serving as a trainer, the Tucano is capable of undertaking strike missions armed with machine-gun pods, rockets or unguided bombs. The Tucano has served against drug organizations, and was used as a strike aircraft by rebels during the 1992 coup attempt in Venezuela. The Brazilian air force uses the Tucano as a light strike platform and also for aerobatic displays.

SPECIFICATIONS

COUNTRY OF ORIGIN: Brazil
TYPE: two-seat piston-engined trainer/light strike aircraft
POWERPLANT: one Pratt & Whitney Canada PT6A-25C piston engine
PERFORMANCE: max speed 448kph (278.26mph); initial climb 792m/min (2600 ft/min); ceiling 9150m (30,000ft); range 1844km (1146 miles)

WEIGHT LOADED: 1790kg (3946lbs); maximum takeoff weight 3175kg (7000lbs)
DIMENSIONS: span 11.14m (37ft 7in); length 9.86m (32ft 4in); height 3.4m (12ft 2in)
ARMAMENT: usually none; can carry up to 1000kg (2200lbs) of machine-gun pods, bombs and rockets on four wing pylons

FMA IA 27 Pulqui

The Pulquí (Arrow) was designed by Emile Dewoitine, who had established his own aircraft company in France in 1920. The aircraft achieved two firsts, being not only the first single-seat fighter to be designed in Argentina but also the first turbojet-powered aircraft to be built by her fledgling aviation industry. The aircraft followed a conventional low-wing cantilever monoplane design, constructed of metal, and powered by the Rolls Royce Derwent turbojet. The aircraft first flew on 9 August 1947, but flight trials proved disappointing in every aspect. The project was subsequently abandoned. Enlisting the assistance of former Focke-Wulf designer Kurt Tank, the Argentine government sought to rekindle the project with the Pulquí II, but a protracted development period and the withdrawal of Dr Tank meant that it too was abandoned in 1960.

SPECIFICATIONS

COUNTRY OF ORIGIN: Argentina
TYPE: single-seat fighter
POWERPLANT: one 2268kg (5000lb) Rolls Royce Nene 2 turbojet
PERFORMANCE: maximum speed at 5000m (16,405ft) 1050km/h (652mph); service ceiling 15,000m (49,210ft); endurance 2 hours 12 minutes
WEIGHT LOADED: empty 3600kg (7937lb); maximum take-off 5550kg (12,236lb)
DIMENSIONS: wingspan 10.60m (34ft 9in); length 11.68m (38ft 4in); height 3.50m (11ft 6in); wing area 25.10m^2 (270.18ft^2)
ARMAMENT: four 20mm (0.79in) cannon

FMA IA 63 Pampa

The physical resemblance between the Pampa and the Dassault/Dornier stems from the close association between Argentinian manufacturer FMA and Dornier on the project. Design work began in 1979 to provide a jet trainer to replace the Morane-Saulnier MS.760 Paris in service with the Argentine air force. Wings and tailplanes for the prototype were based on a unswept version of the Alpha Jet wing. Other features were designed for simplified maintenance and cheap operation, such as the aircraft's single-engined configuration and reduced avionics suite. Rough airstrip operations are possible. The first prototype, which is depicted here with its Paris Air Show registration, flew on 6 October 1984. The first of 100 aircraft ordered for the Argentine air force was delivered to IV Brigada Aärea in April 1988.

SPECIFICATIONS

COUNTRY OF ORIGIN: United Kingdom
TYPE: two-seat advanced pilot trainer with combat capability
POWERPLANT: one 1588kg (3500lb) Garrett TFE731-2-2N turbofan
PERFORMANCE: maximum speed 750km/h (466mph); service ceiling 12,900m (42,325ft); combat radius on hi-lo-hi mission with 1000kg (2205lb) load 360km (223 miles)
WEIGHT LOADED: empty 2821kg (6219lb); maximum take-off 5000kg (11,023lb)
DIMENSIONS: wingspan 9.69m (31ft 9in); length (excluding probe) 10.93m (35ft 10in); height 4.29m (14ft 1in); wing area 15.63m^2 (168.2ft^2)
ARMAMENT: provision for a 30mm (1.18in) DEFA cannon and four underwing pylons for up to 1160kg (2557lb) of stores

Fuji T-1A

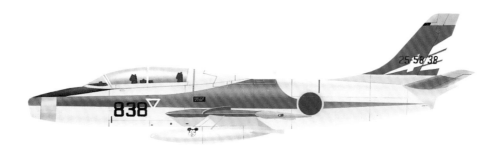

Once the Japanese aircraft industry had been cleared to begin production again in 1953, the government awarded a number of substantial contracts to Fuji with the aim of producing indigenous jet powered aircraft to replace American supplied piston-engined T-6 Texans. The company had already constructed a small turbojet engine to power just such an aircraft, but the first T-1F1 was powered by an imported Bristol Siddeley Orpheus engine. The design leant heavily on the North American F-86 Sabre. Designated T-1A by the JASDF, the Orpheus powered aircraft began to enter service in 1961 and by July of the following year 40 had been delivered. The company also produced a T-1B version, powered, or rather underpowered, by the Japan Jet Engine Co. J3-3. This engine delivered only two-thirds of the thrust of the Bristol engine.

SPECIFICATIONS

COUNTRY OF ORIGIN: Japan
TYPE: two-seat intermediate jet trainer
POWERPLANT: one 1814kg (4000lb) Rolls Royce (Bristol Siddeley) Orpheus Mk 805 turbojet
PERFORMANCE: maximum speed 925km/h (575mph) at high altitude; service ceiling 14,400m (47,250ft); range 1860km (1156 miles) at high altitude with drop tanks
WEIGHT LOADED: empty 2420kg (5335lb); maximum take-off 5000kg (11,023lb)
DIMENSIONS: wingpsan 10.49m (34ft 5in); length 12.12m (39ft 9in); height 4.08m (13ft 5in); wing area 22.22m^2 (239.2ft^2)
ARMAMENT: optional 12.7mm (0.5in) Browning M53-2 gun in nose; two underwing pylons with provision for up to 680kg (1500lb) of stores, including bombs, Sidewinder air-to-air missiles, or gun pods; usually only tanks carried

General Dynamics F-16A

The F-16 is undoubtedly one of the most important fighter aircraft of the 20th century. It started fairly inauspiciously as a technology demonstrator to see to what degree it would be possible to build a useful fighter that was significantly smaller and cheaper than the F-15 Eagle. The US Air Force termed this the Lightweight Fighter programme and it was not initially intended to lead to a production aircraft. Contracts for two prototypes each of the General Dynamics 401 and Northrop P.530 were awarded in April 1972. Interest in the concept from a number of America's NATO allies led to a total revision of the LWF program; it was subsequently announced that the US Air Force would buy 650 of the successful Air Combat Fighter design. In December 1974 the General Dynamics design was announced as the winner. The first production F-16A was flown on 7 August 1978.

SPECIFICATIONS

COUNTRY OF ORIGIN: United States
TYPE: single-seat air combat and ground attack fighter
POWERPLANT: either one 10,800kg (23,770lb) Pratt & Whitney F100-PW-200 or one 13,150kg (28,984lb) General Electric F110-GE-100 turbofan
PERFORMANCE: maximum speed 2142km/h (1320mph); service ceiling above 15,240m (50,000ft); operational radius 925km (525 miles)
WEIGHT LOADED: empty 7070kg (15,586lb); maximum take-off 16,057kg (35,400lb)
DIMENSIONS: wingspan 9.45m (31ft); length 15.09m (49ft 6in); height 5.09m (16ft 8in); wing area 27.87m^2 (300ft^2)
ARMAMENT: one General Electric M61A1 20mm (0.79in) multi-barrelled cannon, wingtip missile stations; seven external hardpoints with provision for up to 9276kg (20,450lb) of stores, including air-to-air missiles, air-to-surface missiles, ECM pods, reconnaissance or rocket pods, conventional or laser guided bombs, or fuel tanks

General Dynamics F-16B

The F-16B is a two-seat trainer version of General Dynamics' highly successful Fighting Falcon, and shares a physically similar airframe. The second cockpit occupies the area taken up by a fuel tank in the single-seat F-16A. Two of the eight pre-production aircraft were ordered as two-seaters, with the first one flying in August 1977. The USAF has ordered approximately 204 of the two-seat version, and most foreign customers have opted to purchase both types in conjunction. The USAF fleet of F-16A/Bs have undergone a mid-life Multi-national Staged Improvement Program to ensure their effectiveness as combat aircraft into the next century. A further two-seat variant designated the F-16D has been produced, which incorporates the avionics and systems improvements that have been retrofitted to the MSIP F-16A/B aircraft.

SPECIFICATIONS

COUNTRY OF ORIGIN: United States
TYPE: single-seat air combat and ground attack fighter
POWERPLANT: either one 10,800kg (23,770lb) Pratt & Whitney F100-PW-200 or one 13,150kg (28,984lb) General Electric F110-GE-100 turbofan
PERFORMANCE: maximum speed 2142km/h (1320mph); service ceiling above 15,240m (50,000ft); operational radius 925km (525 miles)
WEIGHT LOADED: empty 7070kg (15,586lb); maximum take-off 16,057kg (35,400lb)
DIMENSIONS: wingspan 9.45m (31ft); length 15.09m (49ft 6in); height 5.09m (16ft 8in); wing area 27.87m² (300ft²)
ARMAMENT: one General Electric M61A1 20mm (0.79in) multi-barrelled cannon, wingtip missile stations; seven external hardpoints with provision for up to 9276kg (20,450lb) of stores, including air-to-air missiles (AIM-9 Sidewinder and AIM-120 AMRAAM), air-to-surface missiles, ECM pods, reconnaissance or rocket pods, conventional or laser guided bombs, or fuel tanks

Gloster Meteor F.Mk 8

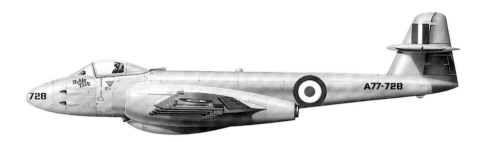

The Gloster Meteor was designed by George Carter to Air Ministry Specification F.9/40. It was the first Allied jet combat design, and the only one to see service during World War II. Trials were carried out with various basic engine types: the Rolls Royce W.2B, the de Havilland developed Halford H.1, and the Metrovick F.2 among them. The first 20 production aircraft were powered by modified W.2B/23C Welland turbojets. The Meteor entered service with No. 616 Squadron on 12 July 1944 and saw action against V-1 flying bombs. The F.Mk 8 was the most prolific variant, with a lengthened fuselage, redesigned tail, and additional 432-litre (95-gal) fuel tank, and a bubble canopy. Later F.Mk 8s also had bigger engine inlets. The aircraft also boasted a gyro-stabilized gunsight and one the first Martin Baker ejection seats. The first of 1183 F.Mk 8s was flown on 12 October 1948.

SPECIFICATIONS

COUNTRY OF ORIGIN: United Kingdom
TYPE: single-seat fighter
POWERPLANT: two 1587kg (3600lb) Rolls Royce Derwent 8 turbojets
PERFORMANCE: maximum speed at 10,000m (33,000ft) 962km/h (598mph); service ceiling 13,106m (43,000ft); range 1580km (980 miles)
WEIGHT LOADED: empty 4820kg (10,626lb); loaded 8664kg (19,100lb)
DIMENSIONS: wingspan 11.32m (37ft 2in); length 13.58m (44ft 7in); height 3.96m (13ft)
ARMAMENT: four 20mm (0.79in) Hispano cannon, foreign F.8s often modified to carry two iron bombs, eight rockets, or other offensive stores

Gloster Meteor NF.Mk 11

The N.F Meteor series were tandem-seat night-fighters. Development work began in 1949, and was carried out by Armstrong Whitworth. It was decided to use the cockpit section of the T.Mk 7 Meteor trainer for the prototype. The T.Mk 7 was originally developed by Gloster as a private venture but subsequently was bought by both the Royal Navy and Royal Air Force. The forward fuselage was extended to accommodate SCR-720 AI Mk 10 radar, which was mated to an F.Mk 8 rear fuselage and tail unit. The wing was similar to that used on the F.Mk 1 but redesigned to house the four 20mm (0.79in) cannon displaced from the nose. This aircraft was the basis of the first Meteor night-fighter, designated N.F.11, which appeared in prototype form on 31 May 1950. One still flies with Jet Heritage Ltd in the UK. Like many other two-seaters, it ended its life as a target tug.

SPECIFICATIONS

COUNTRY OF ORIGIN: United Kingdom
TYPE: twin-seat night-fighter
POWERPLANT: two 1587kg (3,600lb) Rolls-Royce Derwent 8 turbojets
PERFORMANCE: maximum speed at 10,000m (33,000ft) 931km/h (579mph); service ceiling 12,192m (40,000ft); range 1580km (980 miles)
WEIGHT LOADED: empty 5400kg (11,900lb); loaded 9979kg (22,000lb)
DIMENSIONS: wingspan 13.1m (43ft); length 14.78m (48ft 6in); height 4.22m (13ft 10in)
ARMAMENT: four 20mm (0.79in) Hispano cannon

Gloster Meteor PR.Mk 10

The PR.Mk 10 was a specialized photo-reconnaissance version of the Meteor, which followed the FR.Mk 9 into production in 1950. The Mk 10 was something of a hybrid, with the longer wings of early Mk III models, the tail unit of the Mk IV, and the longer fuselage of the Mk 9 carrying a camera nose. Unlike the previous model, the Mk 10 had no armament, and could operate at higher altitude. It also carried vertical cameras, and effectively replaced the Spitfire PR.XIX for strategic reconnaissance at high altitude. The first PR.Mk 10 made its initial flight on 22 March 1950. The Mk 10 entered service with the Royal Air Force with 541 Squadron in January 1951. A total of 58 were produced, along with 126 of the Mk 9s. These were the only two photo-reconnaissance versions built. Note the centreline fuel tank introduced on the F.Mk 8.

SPECIFICATIONS

COUNTRY OF ORIGIN: United Kingdom
TYPE: single-seat photo-reconnaissance aircraft
POWERPLANT: two 1587kg (3600lb) Rolls-Royce Derwent 8 turbojets
PERFORMANCE: maximum speed at 10,000m (33,000ft) 962km/h (598mph); service ceiling 13,106m (43,000ft); range 1580km (980 miles)
WEIGHT LOADED: empty 4895kg (10,970lb); loaded 6946kg (19,100lb)
DIMENSIONS: wingspan 13.1m (43ft); length 13.54m (44ft 3in); height 3.96m (13ft)
ARMAMENT: none

Grumman F-14A Tomcat

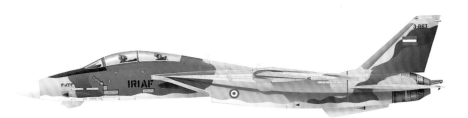

The F-14 was developed largely because of the failure of the F-111B fleet fighter programme, yet has not enjoyed a trouble free service life itself. Continuing problems with the engines have led to escalating maintenance costs (one of the reasons for the development of the cheaper F-18) and a relatively high accident rate. Despite these problems the Tomcat is widely regarded as the finest interceptor flying anywhere in the world. Development of the F-14A was hampered by the loss of the first prototype in December 1970. The aircraft entered service less than two years later with VF-125, before embarking for the first operational tour with VF-1 and VF-2 on USS *Enterprise* in September 1974. The F-14 succeeded the F-4 as the premier fleet defence fighter. A total of 478 F-14As were supplied to the US Navy. Eighty aircraft were exported to Iran from 1976.

SPECIFICATIONS

COUNTRY OF ORIGIN: United States
TYPE: two-seat carrierborne fleet defence fighter
POWERPLANT: two 9480kg (20,900lb) Pratt & Whitney TF30-P-412A turbofans
PERFORMANCE: maximum speed at high altitude 2517km/h (1564mph); service ceiling 17,070m (56,000ft); range about 3220km (2000 miles)
WEIGHT LOADED: empty 18,191kg (40,104lb); maximum take-off 33,724kg (74,349lb)
DIMENSIONS: wingspan 19.55m (64ft 1.5in) unswept; 11.65m (38ft 3in) swept; length 19.10m (62ft 8in); height 4.88m (16ft); wing area 52.49m^2 (565ft^2)
ARMAMENT: one 20mm (0.79in) M61A1 Vulcan rotary cannon with 675 rounds; external pylons for a combination of AIM-7 Sparrow medium range air-to-air missiles, AIM-9 medium range air-to-air missiles, and AIM-54 Phoenix long range air-to-air missiles

Grumman F-14D Tomcat

In 1973, the US Navy was forced to curtail development of the first F-14B project, powered by twin 12,741kg (28,090lb) Pratt & Whitney F401-P400 turbofans. The result of the cancellation was that all production F-14As were fitted with the TF30, which had only ever been designed as an interim engine. In 1984 it was decided to develop an interim improved version of the F-14 with General Electric F110-GE- 400, designated the F-14A (Plus). Thirty-two aircraft were converted and later designated F-14B. The F-14D project suffered a seemingly endless round of cancellations and reinstatements prior to the funding of 37 new-build aircraft and 18 rebuilds from F-14As. The F-14D benefits from an improved version of the powerful APG-70 radar, the APG-71, redesign of the cockpit instrumentation, improved defensive suite and tactical jamming system.

SPECIFICATIONS

COUNTRY OF ORIGIN: United States
TYPE: two-seat carrierborne fleet defence fighter
POWERPLANT: two 12,247kg (27,000lb) General Electric F110-GE-400 turbofans
PERFORMANCE: maximum speed at high altitude 1988km/h (1241mph); service ceiling 16,150m (53,000ft); range about 1994km (1239 miles) with full weapon load
WEIGHT LOADED: empty 18,951kg (41,780lb); maximum take-off 33,724kg (74,349lb)
DIMENSIONS: wingspan 19.55m (64ft 2in) unswept; 11.65m (38ft 3in) swept; length 19.10m (62ft 8in); height 4.88m (16ft); wing area 52.49m^2 (565ft^2)
ARMAMENT: one 20mm (0.79in) M61A1 Vulcan rotary cannon with 675 rounds; external pylons for a combination of AIM-7 Sparrow medium range air-to-air missiles, AIM-9 medium range air-to-air missiles, and AIM-54A/B/C Phoenix long range air-to-air missiles

Hawker Hunter F.Mk 1

Without question the most successful post-war British fighter aircraft, the Hunter has a grace and elegance that complements its effectiveness as a warplane. It is fondly remembered by a generation of pilots who delighted in its superb handling characteristics. The first production F.Mk 1 entered service in July 1954; the aircraft was produced in dozens of different guises, and enjoyed a service career across the globe that spanned 40 years. The F.Mk 1 was easily supersonic in a shallow dive and packed a devastating punch with four 30mm (1.18in) Aden cannon in a quick-release pack winched up as a unit. One early problem on this otherwise vicefree aircraft was the tendency for the Avon 100 engine to stop when the guns were fired! On 7 September 1953, the one-off Mk 3 raised the world speed record to 727.6mph off the Sussex coast, piloted by Squadron Leader Neville Duke.

SPECIFICATIONS

COUNTRY OF ORIGIN: United Kingdom
TYPE: single-seat fighter
POWERPLANT: one 2925kg (6500lb) Rolls-Royce Avon 100 turbojet
PERFORMANCE: maximum speed at sea level 1144km/h (710mph); service ceiling 15,240m (50,000ft); range on internal fuel 689km (490 miles)
WEIGHT LOADED: empty 5501kg (12,128lb); loaded 7347kg (16,200lb)
DIMENSIONS: wingspan 10.26m (33ft 8in); length 13.98m (45ft 10in); height 4.02m (13ft 2in); wing area 32.42m^2 (349ft^2)
ARMAMENT: four 30mm (1.18in) Aden cannon; underwing pylons with provision for two 454kg (1000lb) bombs and 24 76.2mm (3in) rockets

Hawker Hunter T.Mk 8M

In 1953 Hawker began to develop a dual seat trainer version of the Hunter. In July 1955, the prototype P.1101 was flown; production aircraft were designated T.Mk 7 and began entering service with the Royal Air Force in 1958. From this, a sub-series was derived for naval use called the T.Mk 8. Naval trainer versions can be distinguished by the arrestor hook under the rear fuselage. Common to all trainer versions was the enlarged cockpit with side-by-side seating and dual controls, and an enlarged dorsal fairing. Production total for the T.Mk 8 was 41. Both the Defence Evaluation and Research Agency and the Empire Test Pilot's School still operate the aircraft. Two-seat trainer aircraft were supplied under a variety of designations to Denmark, Peru, India, Jordan, Lebanon, Kuwait, Switzerland, Iraq, Chile, Singapore, Abu Dhabi, Qatar and Kenya.

SPECIFICATIONS

COUNTRY OF ORIGIN: United Kingdom
TYPE: dual-seat advanced trainer
POWERPLANT: one 3428kg (8000lb) Rolls-Royce Avon 122 turbojet
PERFORMANCE: maximum speed at sea level 1117km/h (694mph); service ceiling 14,325m (47,000ft); range on internal fuel 689km (429 miles)
WEIGHT LOADED: empty 6406kg (14,122lb); loaded 7802kg (17,200lb)
DIMENSIONS: wingspan 10.26m (33ft 8in); length 14.89m (48ft 10in); height 4.02m (13ft 2in); wing area 32.42m² (349ft²)
ARMAMENT: two 30mm (1.18in) Aden cannon with 150 rounds

Hawker Sea Hawk FGA Mk 6

Although the design of the bifurcated jet pipe caused some concern among defence staff when the prototype P.1040 was first unveiled, Sidney Camm's Sea Hawk has a well earned reputation as a reliable, good handling fighter. The final production version of the Sea Hawk was designated FGA Mk 6, equipped with the more powerful Rolls Royce Nene 103 but otherwise similar to the F.Mk 4. Earlier versions of the Sea Hawk saw action with the Fleet Air Arm during the Suez crisis. Hawker actually built only 35 F.1 Sea Hawks. The remainder were constructed by Armstrong Whitworth who built all 87 of the FGA Mk 6 version. The aircraft remained in service with the FAA until 1960. In 1959 the Indian Navy ordered 24 aircraft similar to the Mk 6. Some were new-build and the rest were refurbished ex-RN Mk 6s.

SPECIFICATIONS

COUNTRY OF ORIGIN: United Kingdom
TYPE: single-seat carrier based fighter-bomber
POWERPLANT: one 2449kg (5400lb) Rolls Royce Nene 103 turbojet
PERFORMANCE: maximum speed at sea level 969km/h (602mph); service ceiling 13,565m (44,500ft); combat radius (clean) 370km (230 miles)
WEIGHT LOADED: empty 4409kg (9720lb); maximum take-off 7348kg (16,200lb)
DIMENSIONS: wingspan 11.89m (39ft); length 12.09m (39ft 8in); height 2.64m (8ft 8in); wing area 25.83m^2 (278ft^2)
ARMAMENT: four 20mm (0.79in) Hispano cannon; plus underwing hardpoints with provision for four 227kg (500lb) bombs, or two 227kg (500lb) bombs and 20 76.2mm (3in) or 16 127mm (5in) rockets

Hawker Sea Hawk Mk 50

The qualities of the Sea Hawk were early on recognised by a number of foreign naval air services leading to the production of export versions. The Mk 50 was an export version of the Sea Hawk F.Mk 6 for the Royal Netherlands Navy. Some 22 were delivered between 1956–57 and they remained in service until the end of 1964, serving on board the carrier Karel Doorman. The Sea Hawk also went for export to India, which was the last remaining operator of the type. This aircraft is a Mk 50 of No. 860 Squadron, Royal Netherlands Navy, distinguished by the broad blade aerial on top of the fuselage. Note the squadron's emblem on the forward fuselage. The unit operated the Sea Hawk during its entire service with the RNN. The Dutch aircraft had provision for Sidewinder 1A air-to-air guided missiles.

SPECIFICATIONS

COUNTRY OF ORIGIN: United Kingdom
TYPE: single-seat carrier based fighter-bomber
POWERPLANT: one 2449kg (5400lb) Rolls Royce Nene 103 turbojet
PERFORMANCE: maximum speed at sea level 969km/h (602mph); service ceiling 13,565m (44,500ft); combat radius (clean) 370km (230 miles)
WEIGHT LOADED: empty 4409kg (9720lb); maximum take-off 7348kg (16,200lb)
DIMENSIONS: wingspan 11.89m (39ft); length 12.09m (39ft 8in); height 2.64m (8ft 8in); wing area 25.83m^2 (278ft^2)
ARMAMENT: four 20mm (0.79in) Hispano cannon; plus underwing hardpoints with provision for four 227kg (500lb) bombs, or two 227kg (500lb) bombs and 20 76.2mm (3in) or 16 127mm (5in) rockets

Hawker Siddeley Gnat T.Mk 1

British designer W.E.W. 'Teddy' Petter planned the Gnat to reverse the trend towards larger and more complex combat aircraft, considering a simple lightweight fighter would offer equal performance at a much lower cost. Folland Aircraft proceeded to fund a private venture prototype known as the Midge and eventually gained an order for a development batch of six, the first of which flew in May 1956. India signed a licence agreement in September 1956 and built 213 at Hindustan Aircraft Ltd at Bangalore. With the knowledge that the RAF was seeking to replace its de Havilland Vampire trainer aircraft Folland funded a further private venture to incorporate a dual seat cockpit. A new wing was designed, the fuselage lengthened, and the control surfaces revised. This aircraft entered service as the Gnat T.Mk 1, which served as the RAF's advanced jet trainer.

SPECIFICATIONS

COUNTRY OF ORIGIN: United Kingdom
TYPE: two-seat advanced trainer
POWERPLANT: one 1134kg (2500lb) Bristol Siddeley Viper Mk 202 turbojet
PERFORMANCE: maximum speed at 7620m (25,000ft) 708km/h (440mph); service ceiling 11,185m (36,700ft); maximum range with tip tanks 1448km (900 miles)
WEIGHT LOADED: maximum take-off with tip tanks 4173kg (9200lb)
DIMENSIONS: wingspan 10.77m (35ft 4in); length 10.36m (34ft); height 3.10m (10ft 2in); wing area 19.85m^2 (213.7ft^2)
ARMAMENT: none

Hunting (Percival) P.84 Jet Provost

In the early 1950s the RAF were continuing to train pilots for fast jet operations on the piston engined Percival Provost. This situation was less than ideal; Hunting recognised the likelihood of an RAF requirement for a basic jet trainer and developed the Jet Provost as a private venture in response. The prototype retained the wings and tail unit of the piston engined P.56 Provost, mated to a new fuselage housing the turbine engine and landing gear. The T.Mk 1 first flew on 16 June 1953, and subsequently was built in large numbers for the RAF. The Jet Provost remained in service in three basic versions. The last version, the T.Mk 5, introduced a pressurised cabin, lengthened nose to house avionics equipment, and strengthened wings with increased internal fuel capacity. This was the RAF's basic trainer until 1989, when it was replaced by the Short Tucano.

SPECIFICATIONS

COUNTRY OF ORIGIN: United Kingdom
TYPE: two-seat basic trainer
POWERPLANT: one 1134kg (2500lb) Bristol Siddeley Viper Mk 202 turbojet
PERFORMANCE: maximum speed at 7620m (25,000ft) 708km/h (440mph); service ceiling 11,185m (36,700ft); maximum range with tip tanks 1448km (900 miles)
WEIGHT LOADED: maximum take-off with tip tanks 4173kg (9200lb)
DIMENSIONS: wingspan 10.77m (35ft 4in); length 10.36m (34ft); height 3.10m (10ft 2in); wing area 19.85m² (213.7ft²)
ARMAMENT: none

IAI Kfir C1

During the 1950s, Israel was forced to rely almost solely on France for procurement of combat aircraft. The original Mirage IIIC actually owes much of its inception to the close ties between Dassault and Israel. During the Six Day War of 5–10 June 1967 this aircraft performed magnificently, yet Dassault was informed by an irate General de Gaulle that he could not deliver the improved Mirage 5 attack aircraft which had been developed for Israel and already paid for. Israeli Aircraft Industries were thus directed to concentrate their energies on making Israel more self-sufficient in combat aircraft, and to devise an improved version of the Mirage III. The company adapted the airframe to take a General Electric J79 turbojet, under a programme dubbed Black Curtain. Some of these aircraft participated in the 1973 Yom Kippur war.

SPECIFICATIONS

COUNTRY OF ORIGIN: Israel
TYPE: single-seat interceptor
POWERPLANT: one 8119kg (17,900lb) General Electric J79-J1E turbojet
PERFORMANCE: maximum speed above 11,000m (36,090ft) 2445km/h (1,520mph); service ceiling 17,680m (58,000ft); combat radius as interceptor 346km (215 miles)
WEIGHT LOADED: empty 7285kg (16,090lb); maximum take-off 16,200kg (35,715lb)
DIMENSIONS: wingspan 8.22m (26ft 11in); length 15.65m (51ft 4in); height 4.55m (14ft 11in); wing area 34.80m² (374.60ft²)
ARMAMENT: one IAI (DEFA) 30mm (1.18in) cannon; nine external hardpoints with provision for up to 5775kg (12,732lb) of stores; for interception duties AIM-9 Sidewinder air-to-air missiles, or indigenously produced AAMs such as the Shafrir or Python

IAI Kfir C2

The C2 was the major production version of the Kfir, and was first publicly demonstrated on 20 July 1976. Improvements included the adoption of small removable swept canard foreplanes on the inlet trunks to improve flying characteristics, a small strake on each side of the nose, and extended chord (breadth) outer wings to improve take-off, landing and general combat performance. Later aircraft in the run of 185 (including TC2 trainer aircraft) were fitted with an improved radar system. Between 1983-85 most C2s were upgraded to C7 standard, with improved engine thrust and avionics, and two additional external stores pylons. None remain in service with the IDF. The aircraft was also supplied to Colombia. This aircraft was based at Hatzerim in the Negev desert, and wears standard IDF/AF camouflage.

SPECIFICATIONS

COUNTRY OF ORIGIN: Israel
TYPE: single-seat interceptor/ground attack aircraft
POWERPLANT: one 8119kg (17,900lb) General Electric J79-J1E turbojet
PERFORMANCE: maximum speed above 11,000m (36,090ft) 2445km/h (1,520mph); service ceiling 17,680m (58,000ft); combat radius as interceptor 346km (215 miles)
WEIGHT LOADED: empty 7285kg (16,090lb); maximum take-off 16,200kg (35,715lb)
DIMENSIONS: wingspan 8.22m (26ft 11in); length 15.65m (51ft 4in); height 4.55m (14ft 11in); wing area 34.80m^2 (374.60ft^2)
ARMAMENT: one IAI (DEFA) 30mm (1.18in) cannon; nine external hardpoints with provision for up to 5775kg (12,732lb) of stores; for ground attack duties a wide range of stores, including conventional and guided bombs, cluster bombs, rockets, napalm tanks, air-to-ground missiles

Lockheed F-94A Starfire

Retaining many of the features of the F-80 and T-33 aircraft from which it was developed, the tandem-seat Starfire was conceived in 1949 a radar equipped all-weather interceptor. Two prototypes were produced by converting existing T-33 airframes. Changes included the installation of a 2724kg (6000lb) Allison J33-A-33 afterburning turbojet, remodelling the nose to accommodate radar, and revised accommodation for the pilot and radar operator. The first flight took place on 1 July 1949, and production of 110 similar F-94As began the same year. The first deliveries, to the 319th All Weather Fighter Squadron began in June 1950. Two improved variants were produced, the F-94B with a blind landing system and raised tip tanks, and the F-94C, with redesigned wing and fin, longer fuselage, more powerful engine, and 24 Mighty Mouse unguided air-to-air rockets in the nose.

SPECIFICATIONS

COUNTRY OF ORIGIN: United States
TYPE: tandem-seat all-weather interceptor
POWERPLANT: one 2724kg (6000lb) Allison J33-A-33 turbojet
PERFORMANCE: maximum speed at 30,000ft 933km/h (580mph); service ceiling 14,630m (48,000ft); range 1850km/h (1150 miles)
WEIGHT LOADED: empty 5030kg (11,090lb); maximum take-off 7125kg (15,710lb)
DIMENSIONS: wingspan not including tip tanks 11.85m (38ft 11in); length 12.2m (40ft 1in); height 3.89m (12ft 8in); wing area 22.13m^2 (238ft^2)
ARMAMENT: four 12.7mm (0.5in) machine guns

Lockheed F-104G Starfighter

The F-104G was a complete redesign of the Starfighter to meet the needs of the Luftwaffe for a tactical nuclear strike and reconnaissance aircraft. This aircraft was developed especially for export to client countries and was first flown in prototype form in June 1960. By comparison with the F-104D the 'F' had a substantially strengthened fuselage, and boasted Nasarr multi-mode radar, inertial navigation system, manoeuvring flaps and other improvements. Ninety-six were supplied to the Luftwaffe who deployed them in a number of different roles. The aircraft pictured carries the MBB Kormoran anti-ship missile and was operated by the Marine Hieger. Some 184 RF-104Gs, which is a tactical reconnaissance version of the Starfighter were constructed. Italy and Germany were among the last major operators of the aircraft.

SPECIFICATIONS

COUNTRY OF ORIGIN: United States
TYPE: single-seat multi-mission strike fighter
POWERPLANT: one 7076kg (15,600lb) General Electric J79-GE-11A turbojet
PERFORMANCE: maximum speed at 15,240m (50,000ft) 1845km/h (1146mph); service ceiling 15,240m (50,000ft); range 1740km (1081 miles)
WEIGHT LOADED: empty 6348kg (13,995lb); maximum take-off 13,170kg (29,035lb)
DIMENSIONS: wingspan (excluding missiles) 6.36m (21ft 9in); length 16.66m (54ft 8in); height 4.09m (13ft 5in); wing area 18.22m^2 (196.10ft^2)
ARMAMENT: one 20mm (0.79in) General Electric M61A1 cannon, provision for AIM-9 Sidewinder on fuselage, under wings or on tips, and/or stores up to a maximum of 1814kg (4000lb)

Lockheed F-117 Night Hawk

The F-117 is probably the most important aircraft to enter service in the past two decades, and has redefined our concept of what the flying machine of the 21st century will look like. The development program is shrouded in secrecy, but it is likely that research into stealth technology began in earnest in the wake of a number of successful radar guided missile attacks on US built F-4s during the 1973 Yom Kippur war. Both Lockheed and Northrop submitted proposals for the Experimental Stealth Technology requirement issued by the DOD; Lockheed's proposal was subsequently selected in 1977 and the plane was delivered five years later. In the 1991 Gulf war the Night Hawk really hit the headlines. Exploiting the low radar visibility, pilots were able to penetrate Iraqi airspace undetected and deliver useful quantities of ordnance with pinpoint accuracy.

SPECIFICATIONS

COUNTRY OF ORIGIN: United States
TYPE: single-seat stealth attack aircraft
POWERPLANT: two 4899kg (10,800lb) General Electric F404-GE-F1D2 turbofans
PERFORMANCE: maximum speed about Mach 1at high altitude: combat radius about 1112km (691 miles) with maximum payload
WEIGHT LOADED: empty about 13,608kg (30,000lb); maximum take-off 23,814kg (52,500lb)
DIMENSIONS: wingspan 13.20m (43ft 4in); length 20.08m (65ft 11in); height 3.78m (12ft 5in); wing area about 105.9m^2 (1140ft^2)
ARMAMENT: provision for 2268kg (5000lb) of stores on rotary dispenser in weapon bay; including the AGM-88 HARM anti-radiation missile; AGM-65 Maverick ASM, GBU-19 and GBU-27 optronically guided bombs, BLU-109 laser-guided bomb, and B61 free-fall nuclear bomb

Lockheed P-80A Shooting Star

The P-80A was the first production model of the Shooting Star. The lettered prefix was later changed from 'P' (Pursuit) to 'F' (Fighter) due to changes in the American designation system in 1947. The aircraft pictured 44-85226 'Betsy Jean' is adorned with the vertical coloured stripes of the commander of the 412th Fighter Group. This type of national insignia and the PN buzz-code was used until 1947, when the USAF became an independent service. In June 1947, Colonel Alfred Boyd flew a modified P-80R to a new world speed record of 1003.8 km/h (623.8mph) at Muroc Dry Lake, California. The aircraft was also subject to a great deal of experimentation, with various armament and propulsion packages tried at various points throughout its service life. Many aircraft ended their days as unmanned target drones.

SPECIFICATIONS

COUNTRY OF ORIGIN: United States
TYPE: single-seat fighter bomber
POWERPLANT: one 1746kg (3850lb) Allison J33-GE-11 turbojet
PERFORMANCE: maximum speed at sea level 966km/h (594mph); service ceiling 14,265m (46,800ft); range 1328km (825 miles)
WEIGHT LOADED: empty 3819kg (8420lb); maximum take-off 7646kg (16,856lb)
DIMENSIONS: wingspan 11.81m (38ft 9in); length 10.49m (34ft 5in); height 3.43m (11ft 3in); wing area 22.07m^2 (237.6ft^2)
ARMAMENT: six 12.7mm (0.5in) machine guns, plus two 454kg (1000lb) bombs and eight rockets

Lockheed T-1A SeaStar

The final variant in the F-80/T-33/F-94 family was the T2V-1 SeaStar jet trainer, an advanced version of the T-33A two seat trainer aircraft. The navalised version of this aircraft was designated the TV-2, and featured arrestor gear for carrier landings. The T2V-1 (later T1-A) was a further refinement, with humped cockpit, leading and trailing edge flaps, boundary layer control and a 2769kg (6100lb) Allison turbojet. Nearly 700 T2-V aircraft were produced for the US Navy and it served for a considerable time as their standard trainer aircraft. The aircraft pictured served with the US Navy Test Pilot School in Maryland during the 1960s, until replaced by the Northrop T-38 Talon. The red/white colour scheme has been standard for US Navy trainers since the 1950s. Some SeaStars have been converted for use as avionics test beds.

SPECIFICATIONS

COUNTRY OF ORIGIN: United States
TYPE: two-seat jet trainer
POWERPLANT: one 2769kg (6100lb) Allison J33-A-35 turbojet
PERFORMANCE: maximum speed at 7620m (25,000ft) 879km/h (546mph); service ceiling 14,630m (48,000ft); endurance 3 hours 7 minutes
WEIGHT LOADED: empty 3667kg (8084lb); maximum take-off 6551kg (14,442lb)
DIMENSIONS: wingspan 11.85m (38ft 11in); length 11.51m (37ft 10in); height 3.56m (11ft 8in); wing area 21.81m² (234.8ft²)
ARMAMENT: none

Lockheed T-33A

Longest serving of all Shooting Star variants was the T-33 trainer conversion, produced by lengthening a standard F-80C airframe by more than a metre to accommodate a second seat beneath a single canopy. The first conversion, designated TF-80C, flew on 22 March 1948. The aircraft was adopted as the standard jet trainer of the US Air Force, and found a ready market overseas. Many were supplied to US allies under the Military Assistance Program. Production by Lockheed continued until August 1959, by which time a total of 5691 had been built. The aircraft has been adapted for many other roles; the QT-33 target drone perhaps the most important of these conversions. A version for service with smaller air forces had armament revision making it suitable for weapons training and counter-insurgency.

SPECIFICATIONS

COUNTRY OF ORIGIN: United States
TYPE: two-seat jet trainer
POWERPLANT: one 2449kg (5400lb) Allison J33-A-35 turbojet
PERFORMANCE: maximum speed at 7620m (25,000ft) 879km/h (546mph); service ceiling 14,630m (48,000ft); endurance 3 hours 7 minutes
WEIGHT LOADED: empty 3667kg (8084lb); maximum take-off 6551kg (14,442lb)
DIMENSIONS: wingspan 11.85m (38ft 11in); length 11.51m (37ft 10in); height 3.56m (11ft 8in); wing area 21.81m^2 (234.8ft^2)
ARMAMENT: two 0.5mm (0.02in) machine guns; wide variety of ordnance in COIN role

Lockheed/Boeing F-22 Raptor

In April 1991, after a tightly fought competition to find a replacement for the F-15 Eagle, the Pratt & Whitney powered F-22 proposed by the Lockheed/ Boeing partnership was declared the winner. The aircraft will incorporate all of the most advanced avionics and airframe technology at the disposal of the two companies, such as stealth, a long-range supersonic combat radius, high agility and STOL capability, and an advanced navigation/attack system using artificial intelligence to filter data and so reduce the pilot's workload. The definitive airframe design was achieved in March 1992. The USAF plan to buy 648 aircraft, at a cost of $59.4 million each. Early in the next century the Raptor will begin replacing the F-15 Eagle as the USAF's premier air combat fighter. Flight testing is proceeding well, despite the loss of the second prototype (N22YX) in April 1992.

SPECIFICATIONS

COUNTRY OF ORIGIN: United States
TYPE: single-seat supersonic air superiority fighter
POWERPLANT: two 15,876kg (35,000lb) Pratt & Whitney F119-P-100 turbofans
PERFORMANCE: maximum speed 2335km/h (1451mph); service ceiling 19,812m (65,000ft); combat radius 1285km (800miles)
WEIGHT LOADED: empty 14,061kg (31,000lb); maximum take-off 27,216 kg (60,000lb)
DIMENSIONS: wingspan 13.1m (43ft); length 19.55m (64ft 2in); height 5.39m (17ft 8in); wing area 77.1m^2 (830ft^2)
ARMAMENT: production aircraft will have cannon armament plus next generation air-to-air missiles in the internal weapons bay

Lockheed Martin F-35A Lightning II

The Lightning II was developed as the 'Joint Strike Fighter' project to meet the needs of several international operators. Three variants are available; a conventional takeoff and landing (CTOL) model for air force use, a short takeoff and vertical landing (STOVL) version for the US Marine Corps and the Royal Navy, and a carrier-capable variant for the US Navy. Despite significant differences between the versions, 70–90 per cent of parts are common, simplifying the support and maintenance equation. The Lightning incorporates low-observable ('stealth') technologies to enhance survivability. It can carry a limited armament internally – in two bays forward of the landing gear – to reduce radar return. Additional weapons can be carried on external pylons, at the price of increasing radar return. The conventional F-35A model mounts an internal 25mm cannon. The B and C variants can carry a cannon in an external pod.

SPECIFICATIONS

COUNTRY OF ORIGIN: United States
TYPE: single-seat multirole fighter/attack aircraft
POWERPLANT: one 164.6kN (37,003lbf) Pratt & Whitney F135 afterburning turbofan
PERFORMANCE: maximum speed: Mach 1.6; 2065kph (1,283mph); initial climb: classified; ceiling: 18,288m (60,000ft); range: 2222km (1200nm)
WEIGHT LOADED: empty: 13,300kg (29,300lbs); maximum: 27,216kg (60,000lbs)
DIMENSIONS: span: 10.67m (35ft); length: 15.67m (51ft 4in); height 4.6m (15ft 1in) on internal fuel
ARMAMENT: one 27mm (1.06in) cannon; two AIM-120 AMRAAM; 8164kg (18,000lbs) additional stores

McDonnell F-101B Voodoo

The F-101B was a two-seat all-weather long-range interceptor version of the Voodoo, accommodating a pilot and radar operator to work the MG-13 fire control system and more powerful engines. By fitting a tandem cockpit the company were forced to sacrifice internal fuel capacity, with the subsequent detrimental effect on combat range. An attempt to counter this problem was made by adding an inflight refuelling system. A total of 407 were built, with final delivery taking place in March 1961. In September 1962, McDonnell was awarded a contract to bring 153 F-101Bs up to F-101F standard by updating the fire control system and removing the inflight refuelling probe, amongst other modifications. This aircraft served with the 179th Fighter Interceptor Squadron of the Minnesota ANG at Deluth in 1973.

SPECIFICATIONS

COUNTRY OF ORIGIN: United States
TYPE: two-seat all-weather long-range interceptor
POWERPLANT: two 7672kg (16,900lb) Pratt & Whitney J57-P-55 turbojets
PERFORMANCE: maximum speed at 12190m (40,000ft) 1965km/h (1221mph); service ceiling 16,705m (54,800ft); range 2494km (1550 miles)
WEIGHT LOADED: empty 13,141kg (28,970lb); maximum take-off 23,768kg (52,400lb)
DIMENSIONS: wingspan 12.09m (39ft 8in); length 20.54m (67ft 5in); height 5.49m (18ft); wing area 34.19m^2 (368ft^2)
ARMAMENT: two Mb-1 Genie missiles with nuclear warheads and four AIM-4C,-4D, or 4G Falcon missiles, or six Falcon missiles

McDonnell F2H-2 Banshee

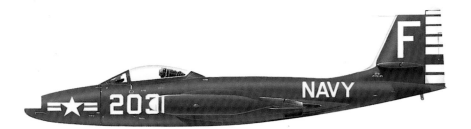

The success of the FH-1 Phantom in US Navy and Marine Corps service meant that it was almost inevitable that McDonnell would be asked to submit a design to succeed the Phantom in service. The Banshee design team under G.V. Covington kept to a broadly similar configuration to the aircraft's predecessor, with a low midset unswept wing, tricycle landing gear. The new aircraft was larger, incorporating folding wings and a lengthened fuselage to accommodate more fuel, and more powerful engines in fattened wing roots. The aircraft was initially designated F-2D, later F2H, and finally F-2. The first F2H-1 aircraft was delivered to the Navy in August 1948, and was followed into service by seven sub-variants. Almost all of the aircraft saw service in Korea, in a wide variety of roles. The F2H-2 was the second production version, with wingtip fuel tanks. Production total was 56.

SPECIFICATIONS

COUNTRY OF ORIGIN: United States
TYPE: carrier-based all-weather fighter
POWERPLANT: one 1474kg (3250lb) Westinghouse J34-WE-34 turbojet
PERFORMANCE: maximum cruising speed 933km/h (580mph); service ceiling 14,205m (46,600ft); combat range 1883km (1170 miles)
WEIGHT LOADED: empty 5980kg (13,183lb); maximum take-off 11,437kg (25,214lb)
DIMENSIONS: wingspan 12.73m (41ft 9in); length 14.68m (48ft 2in); height 4.42m (14ft 6in); wing area 27.31m² (294ft²)
ARMAMENT: four 20mm (0.79in) cannon; underwing racks with provision for two 227kg (500lb) or four 113kg (250lb) bombs

McDonnell F3H-2 Demon

The F3H program was expected to give the US Navy a fighter at least as good as any USAF aircraft, but ultimately proved hugely costly and difficult. Despite the advanced airframe design, serious obstacles were encountered at an early stage. Chief amongst these problems was the failure of the Westinghouse XJ40 engine specifically designed for the aircraft which proved unreliable and unable to deliver sufficient thrust. The problems were compounded by the US Navy, who requested that the aircraft be redesigned as an all-weather night-fighter. The first production F3H-1N aircraft had a substitute J40-WE-22 turbojet, but after 11 accidents (two of them fatal), production was halted. The situation was resolved by installing the Allison J71 turbojet, and the F3H-1 aircraft were either used as ground trainers or retrofitted with the J71. Initial deliveries of the F3H-2 were made to VF-14 in 1956.

SPECIFICATIONS

COUNTRY OF ORIGIN: United States
TYPE: carrier-based strike fighter
POWERPLANT: one 6350kg (14,000lb) Allison J71-A-2E turbojet
PERFORMANCE: maximum cruising speed 1041km/h (647mph); service ceiling 13,000m (42,650ft); combat range 2200km (1370 miles)
WEIGHT LOADED: empty 10,039kg (22,133lb); maximum take-off 15,377kg (33,900lb)
DIMENSIONS: wingspan 10.77m (35ft 4in); length 17.96m (58ft 11in); height 4.44m (14ft 7in); wing area 48.22m^2 (519ft^2)
ARMAMENT: four 20mm (0.79in)cannon; four underwing pylons with provision for up to 2722kg (6000lb) of stores, including bombs and rockets

McDonnell FH-1 Phantom

In 1942 the Bureau of Aeronautics entrusted McDonnell, at that time a relatively new and inexperienced aircraft manufacturer, with the task of designing and building the two prototypes of what would become the US Navy's first carrierbased turbojet-powered single-seat fighter. The resulting prototypes were low-wing monoplanes, with retractable landing gear, with power provided by two turbojets buried in the wing roots. The first flight on 26 January 1945, was made under the power of only one of these engines, as Westinghouse had been unable to deliver the second in sufficient time. Evaluation with the US Navy followed, during which the aircraft became the first US jet to be launched and recovered from an aircraft carrier. An initial contract for 100 FD-1s was placed, although the designation was changed to FH-1 before deliveries began in January 1947.

SPECIFICATIONS

COUNTRY OF ORIGIN: United States
TYPE: carrier-based fighter
POWERPLANT: two 726kg (1600lb) Westinghouse J30-WE-20 turbojets
PERFORMANCE: maximum cruising speed 771km/h (479mph); service ceiling 12,525m (41,100ft); combat range 1118km (695 miles)
WEIGHT LOADED: empty 3031kg (6683lb); maximum take-off 5459kg (12,035lb)
DIMENSIONS: wingspan 12.42m (40ft 9in); length 11.35m (37ft 3in); height 4.32m (14ft 2in); wing area 24.64m^2 (276ft^2)
ARMAMENT: four 12.7mm (0.5in) machine-guns

McDonnell Douglas CF-18A Hornet

On 10 April 1980, the Canadian Armed Forces minister announced his country's decision to buy 138 single-seat F-18A and 40 tandem seat F-18B aircraft, to replace its ageing CF-104 Starfighters. The order for the single-seat F-18A was progressively cut back to 98, but deliveries of trainer aircraft, designated CF-18B, began in October 1982. Each squadron operates a mixture of the two types, to enhance its multi-role capability. By comparison with the aircraft operated by the US Navy, the CF-18 has different Inertial Landing System, an added spotlight on the port side of the fuselage for ready identification during night formation flying, and provision to carry rocket pods. A comprehensive cold weather survival pack is provided for the pilot/crew. The aircraft pictured carries Sidewinder AAMs on the wingtip rails.

SPECIFICATIONS

COUNTRY OF ORIGIN: United States

TYPE: single-seat multi-mission fighter

POWERPLANT: two 7257kg (16,000lb) General Electric F404-GE-400

PERFORMANCE: maximum speed at 12,190m (40,000ft) 1912km/h (1183mph); combat ceiling about 15,240m (50,000ft); combat radius 740km (460 miles) on escort mission or 1065km (662 miles) in attack role

WEIGHT LOADED: empty 10,455kg (23,050lb); maximum take-off 25,401kg (56,000lb)

DIMENSIONS: wingspan 11.43m (37ft 6in); length 17.07m (56ft); height 4.66m (15ft 4in); wing area 37.16m^2 (400ft^2)

ARMAMENT: one 20mm (0.79in) M61A1 Vulcan six-barrel rotary cannon with 570 rounds, nine external hardpoints with provision for up to 7711kg (17,000lb) of stores, including AIM-7M and AIM-9L air-to-air missiles, air-to-surface missiles, anti-ship missiles, Mk 82 conventional and guided bombs, Hunting BL755 CBU cluster bombs, LAU-5003 rocket pods containing 19 CRV-7 70mm (2.76in) rockets, tanks and ECM pods

McDonnell Douglas F-4C Phantom II

The greatest fighter of the post-war era was designed by McDonnell during the 1950s as part of a private venture study to meet anticipated future needs for an aircraft to replace the McDonnell F3H Demon in US Navy service. Although planned as an attack aircraft with four 20mm (0.79in) guns, it was changed into a very advanced gunless all-weather interceptor with missile armament. In this form it entered service as the F-4A (February 1960). In 1961 the F-4B was compared with Air Force fighters then in service and found to outperform all of them, particularly in terms of weapon load and radar performance. As a result it was ordered in modified form as the F-110, later designated the F-4C. This is generally similar to the F-4B but has dual controls, J79-GE-15 engines and a number of systems changes. A total of 635 were built to equip 16 of the 23 Tactical Air Command Wings.

SPECIFICATIONS

COUNTRY OF ORIGIN: United States
TYPE: two seat all-weather fighter/attack aircraft
POWERPLANT: two 7718kg (17,000lb) General Electric J79-GE-15 turbojets
PERFORMANCE: maximum speed at high altitude 2414km/h (1500mph); service ceiling 18,300m (60,000ft); range on internal fuel with no weapon load 2817km (1750 miles)
WEIGHT LOADED: empty 12,700kg (28,000lb); maximum take-off 26,308kg (58,000lb)
DIMENSIONS: span 11.7m (38ft 5in); length 17.76m (58ft 3in); height 4.96m (16ft 3in); wing area 49.24m² (530ft²)
ARMAMENT: four AIM-7 Sparrow recessed under fuselage; two wing pylons for two AIM-7, or four AIM-9 Sidewinder, provision for 20mm (0.79in) M-61 cannon in external centreline pod; four wing pylons for tanks, bombs, or other stores to a maximum weight of 6219kg (13,500lb)

McDonnell Douglas F-4D Phantom II

Both the F-4C and F-4D enjoyed remarkable service records. In the late 1980s, twenty-odd years after production of the latter aircraft ended, some were still being operated with the Air National Guard and the air forces of Iran and South Korea. The F-4D was a much improved version for the US Air Force, and much better suited to their needs. The F-4C's APQ-100 radar and optical sight were replaced by the APQ-109, which improved bombing accuracy immensely. Pilots complained of the lack of inbuilt gun armament (although a cannon pod could be carried on the centreline pylon), a problem not rectified until the introduction of the F-4E. The Air Force received a total of 793, with deliveries beginning in March 1966. Thirty-two were sold to Iran in 1969, and 18 to the Republic of South Korea in 1972.

SPECIFICATIONS

COUNTRY OF ORIGIN: United States
TYPE: two seat all-weather fighter/attack aircraft
POWERPLANT: two 7718kg (17,000lb) General Electric J79-GE-15 turbojets
PERFORMANCE: maximum speed at high altitude 2414km/h (1500mph); service ceiling 18,300m (60,000ft); range on internal fuel with no weapon load 2817km (1750 miles)
WEIGHT LOADED: empty 12,700kg (28,000lb); maximum take-off 26,308kg (58,000lb)
DIMENSIONS: span 11.7m (38ft 5in); length 17.76m (58ft 3in); height 4.96m (16ft 3in); wing area 49.24m^2 (530ft^2)
ARMAMENT: four AIM-7 Sparrow recessed under fuselage; two wing pylons for two AIM-7, or four AIM-9 Sidewinder, provision for 20mm (0.79in) M-61 cannon in external centreline pod; four wing pylons for tanks, bombs, or other stores to a maximum weight of 6219kg (13,500lb)

McDonnell Douglas F-4E Phantom II

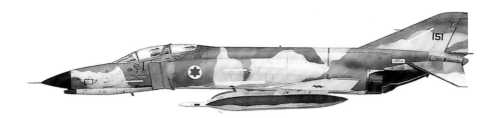

The successes of the Israeli Defence Force/Air Force during the 1973 Yom Kippur war helped to seal the Phantom's reputation as the finest combat aircraft of its generation. Israel purchased 204 F-4Es during the early 1970s, and they remained in front-line operation for many years. Modifications include adoption of the indigenously produced Elta EL/M-2021 multi-mode radar, and it is widely believed that the aircraft were modified to carry the Luz stand-off nuclear weapon. The aircraft pictured is painted in standard 'bleached' two-tone sand and peppermint green with squadron markings carried on the fin. A Shrike antiradiation missile is carried. This weapon helped redress the balance with the SA-2 'guideline' air-to-surface missile, which had caused such devastating losses during the 1967 Six-Day War.

SPECIFICATIONS

COUNTRY OF ORIGIN: United States
TYPE: two-seat all-weather fighter/attack aircraft
POWERPLANT: two 8119kg (17,900lb) General Electric J79-GE-17 turbojets
PERFORMANCE: maximum speed at high altitude 2390km/h (1485mph); service ceiling 19,685m (60,000ft); range on internal fuel with no weapon load 2817km (1750 miles)
WEIGHT LOADED: empty 12,700kg (28,000lb); maximum take-off 26,308kg (58,000lb)
DIMENSIONS: span 11.7m (38ft 5in); length 17.76m (58ft 3in); height 4.96m (16ft 3in); wing area 49.24m^2 (530ft^2)
ARMAMENT: one 20mm (0.79in) M61A1 Vulcan cannon and four AIM-7 Sparrow recessed under fuselage or other weapons up to 1370kg (3020lb) on centreline pylon; four wing pylons for two AIM-7, or four AIM-9 Sidewinder, anti-radiation missiles, bombs, tanks, or other stores up to a maximum weight of 5888kg (12,980lb)

McDonnell Douglas F-4EJ Phantom II

One of the largest operators of the Phantom has been the Japanese Air Self Defence Force. The EJ is a licence-built air-defence version of the F-4E. The original F-4E(J) model was built by McDonnell Douglas (13) and the remainder under licence by Mitsubishi with Kawasaki as a subcontractor (126), with the last delivered in May 1981. The original batch of 45 was then updated to F-4EJ Kai standard with improved weapon and avionics systems such as digital displays, revised Head-Up-Display, fire control system, and nose mounted Texas Instruments AN/APQ-172 radar. The aircraft have a limited lookdown/ shootdown capability with Sparrow and Sidewinder AAMs. The aircraft equipped five squadrons of the JASDF, where they share the air-defence task with McDonnell Douglas F-15 Eagles. Japan also operates an unarmed reconnaissance version of the F-4EJ, designated RF-4EJ.

SPECIFICATIONS

COUNTRY OF ORIGIN: United States
TYPE: two-seat all-weather fighter/attack aircraft
POWERPLANT: two 8119kg (17,900lb) General Electric J79-GE-17 turbojets
PERFORMANCE: maximum speed at high altitude 2390km/h (1485mph); service ceiling 19,685m (60,000ft); range on internal fuel with no weapon load 2817km (1750 miles)
WEIGHT LOADED: empty 12,700kg (28,000lb); maximum take-off 26,308kg (58,000lb)
DIMENSIONS: span 11.7m (38ft 5in); length 17.76m (58ft 3in); height 4.96m (16ft 3in); wing area 49.24m^2 (530ft^2)
ARMAMENT: one 20mm (0.79in) M61A1 Vulcan cannon and four AIM-7 Sparrow recessed under fuselage or other weapons up to 1370kg (3020lb) on centreline pylon; four wing pylons for two AIM-7, or four AIM-9 Sidewinder, for tanks, bombs, or other stores to a maximum weight of 5888kg (12,980lb)

McDonnell Douglas F-4F Phantom II

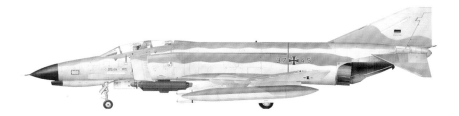

West Germany also enthusiastically adopted the Phantom, initially as a dedicated QRF strike/fighter aircraft, and later solely in the air-defence role. Designation of German-built and operated F-4s is F-4F. Although most airframe parts for the aircraft were manufactured in Germany, final assembly took place in the US. Delivery of the 175 aircraft began during 1975 with completion the following year. One of the major features of the F-4F was the inclusion of leading edge slats to improve low-speed manoeuvring. A simplified APQ-100 radar system replaced the air-to-ground weapons system on the F-4E, which the F-4F otherwise resembles. The aircraft equipped four Jagdgeschwader and Jagdbombergeschwader in the interception and quick reaction strike roles respectively.

SPECIFICATIONS

COUNTRY OF ORIGIN: United States and Germany
TYPE: two-seat all-weather fighter/attack aircraft
POWERPLANT: two 8119kg (17,900lb) General Electric J79-GE-17 turbojets
PERFORMANCE: maximum speed at high altitude 2390km/h (1485mph); service ceiling 19,685m (60,000ft); range on internal fuel with no weapon load 2817km (1750 miles)
WEIGHT LOADED: empty 12,700kg (28,000lb); maximum take-off 26,308kg (58,000lb)
DIMENSIONS: span 11.7m (38ft 5in); length 17.76m (58ft 3in); height 4.96m (16ft 3in); wing area 49.24m^2 (530ft^2)
ARMAMENT: one 20mm (0.79in) M61A1 Vulcan cannon and four AIM-7 Sparrow recessed under fuselage or other weapons up to 1370kg (3020lb) on centreline pylon; four wing pylons for two AIM-7, or four AIM-9 Sidewinder, or four AIM-120 AMRAAM, and/or tanks, bombs, or other stores to a maximum weight of 5888kg (12,980lb)

McDonnell Douglas F-4S Phantom II

One of the lesser known of the F-4 variants, the F-4S was a development of the F-4J models constructed in small numbers for the US Navy. The F-4J had the AWG-10 pulse-doppler radar, drooping ailerons, slatted tail, and J79-GE-10 engines. Also incorporated was an automatic carrier landing system. The F-4S was the redesignation of the remaining aircraft from the original delivery of 12 F-4Js, which were updated with a strengthened structure and leading edge slats. Production of the carrier based Phantoms lasted for a remarkable 17 years. The Phantom was eventually replaced in service by the McDonnell Douglas F/A 18 Hornet. Marine Phantoms were primarily used to support ground units. Pictured here is one of the aircraft operated by UMFA-33 USMC, based at MCAS Beaufort, South Carolina.

SPECIFICATIONS

COUNTRY OF ORIGIN: United States
TYPE: two-seat all-weather fighter/attack carrier-borne aircraft
POWERPLANT: two 8119kg (17,900lb) General Electric J79-GE-10 turbojets
PERFORMANCE: maximum speed at high altitude 2414km/h (1500mph); service ceiling over 18,300m (60,000ft); range on internal fuel with no weapon load 2817km (1750 miles)
WEIGHT LOADED: empty 12,700kg (28,000lb); maximum take-off 26,308kg (58,000lb)
DIMENSIONS: span 11.7m (38ft 5in); length 17.76m (58ft 3in); height 4.96m (16ft 3in); wing area 49.24m² (530ft²)
ARMAMENT: four AIM-7 Sparrow recessed under fuselage; two wing pylons for two AIM-7, or four AIM-9 Sidewinder, provision for 20mm (0.79in) M61A1 cannon in external centreline pod; four wing pylons for tanks, bombs, or other stores to a maximum weight of 6219kg (13,500lb)

McDonnell Douglas F-15A Eagle

To succeed the F-4 Phantom in US service McDonnell Douglas produced the F-15 Eagle. Since its inception, this aircraft has assumed the crown as the world's greatest air superiority fighter, although it has now been superseded by later F-15C and -B variants in US service. The first prototype of the F-15A, a single-seat twin turbofan swept wing aircraft flew in July 1972. The powerful Pratt & Whitney engines and extensive use of titanium in construction (more than twenty percent of the airframe weight of production aircraft) enabled high sustained speeds (Mach 2.5 plus) at high altitude. Impressive flying characteristics became immediately apparent during flight testing, with exceptional time-to-height performance. Deliveries began to the 555th Tactical Fighter Training Wing at Langley AFB, Virginia, in November 1974. Production continued until 1979 with 385 built.

SPECIFICATIONS

COUNTRY OF ORIGIN: United States
TYPE: single-seat air superiority fighter with secondary strike/attack role
POWERPLANT: two 10,885kg (23,810lb) Pratt & Whitney F100-PW-100 turbofans
PERFORMANCE: maximum speed at high altitude 2655km/h (1650mph); initial climb rate over 15,240m (50,000ft)/min; ceiling 30,500m (100,000ft); range on internal fuel 1930km (1200 miles)
WEIGHT LOADED: empty 12,700kg (28,000lb); with maximum load 25,424kg (56,000lb)
DIMENSIONS: wingspan 13.05m (42ft 10in); length 19.43in (63ft 9in); height 5.63m (18ft 5in); wing area 56.48m^2 (608ft^2)
ARMAMENT: one 20mm (0.79in) M61A1 cannon with 960 rounds, external pylons with provision for up to 7620kg (16,800lb) of stores, for example four AIM-7 Sparrow air-to-air missiles and four AIM-9 Sidewinder AAMs; when configured for attack role conventional and guided bombs, rockets, air-to-surface missiles; tanks and/or ECM pods

McDonnell Douglas F-15DJ Eagle

The tandem seat F-15B Eagle was developed alongside the single-seat F-15A, to provide the USAF with a fully conformal trainer version. First flown in July 1973, a little over a year after the F-15A, the F-15B features an extended cockpit to accommodate the student. This was effected with little structural modification, and without changes to the overall airframe dimensions. The complete avionics suite from the F-15A was retained to enable full operational conversion training to be carried out and combat capability to be retained. The F-15DJ is the two-seat version of the F-15C (the upgraded version of the F-15A and the principal production version) for the Japanese Air Self-Defence Force. This aircraft is configured to carry conformal fuel tanks which fit flush with the fuselage, leaving all store hardpoints available for the carriage of weapons. Twelve were delivered.

SPECIFICATIONS

COUNTRY OF ORIGIN: United States

TYPE: twin-seat air superiority fighter trainer with secondary strike/attack role

POWERPLANT: two 10,782kg (23,700lb) Pratt & Whitney F100-PW-220 turbofans

PERFORMANCE: maximum speed at high altitude 2655km/h (1650mph); initial climb rate over 15,240m (50,000ft)/min; ceiling 30,500m (100,000ft); range on internal fuel 4631km (2878 miles)

WEIGHT LOADED: empty 13,336kg (29,400lb); maximum take-off 30,844kg (68,000lb)

DIMENSIONS: wingspan 13.05m (42ft 10in); length 19.43in (63ft 9in); height 5.63m (18ft 5in); wing area 56.48m² (608ft²)

ARMAMENT: one 20mm (0.79in) M61A1 cannon with 960 rounds, external pylons with provision for up to 10,705kg (23,600lb) of stores, for example four AIM-7 Sparrow air-to-air missiles and four AIM-9 Sidewinder AAMs; when configured for attack role conventional and guided bombs, rockets, air-to-surface missiles; tanks and/or ECM pods

McDonnell Douglas F-15J Eagle

By the late 1970s, the USAF had accepted the increasing tactical necessity for an interceptor that could provide top cover during long range strike missions, but defence budget cuts precluded the immediate development of a new aircraft. Instead, the USAF asked McDonnell to adapt the existing F-15A design to include a host of upgrades. The F-15C progressively replaced the F-15A in service with front line USAF units between 1980–89. The most obvious change to the aircraft is the provision for two low-drag conformal fuel tanks (CFTs) that attach to the engine air inlet trunks without affecting the existing external stores stations. The tanks are fitted with stub pylons to allow an extra 5448kg (12,000lb) of stores. Avionics include APG-70 radar, which trebled the processing speed of the APG 63 it replaced. The aircraft was also built under licence in Japan as the F-15J.

SPECIFICATIONS

COUNTRY OF ORIGIN: United States and Japan
TYPE: single-seat strike/attack aircraft and air superiority fighter
POWERPLANT: two 10,782kg (23,770lb) Pratt & Whitney F100-PW-220 turbofans
PERFORMANCE: maximum speed at high altitude 2655km/h (1,650mph); initial climb rate over 15,240m (50,000ft)/min; ceiling 30,500m (100,000ft); range with conformal fuel tanks 5745km (3570 miles)
WEIGHT LOADED: empty 12,793kg (23,770lb); maximum take-off 30,844kg (68,000lb)
DIMENSIONS: wingspan 13.05m (42ft 10in); length 19.43in (63ft 9in); height 5.63m (18ft 5in); wing area 56.48m^2 (608ft^2)
ARMAMENT: one 20mm (0.79in) M61A1 cannon with 960 rounds, external pylons with provision for up to 10,705kg (23,600lb) of stores, typically four AIM-7 Sparrow air-to-air missiles and four AIM-9 Sidewinder AAMs, or eight AIM-120A AMRAAMs; many combinations of conventional and guided bombs, rockets, air-to-surface missiles; tanks and/or ECM pods

McDonnell Douglas F/A-18A Hornet

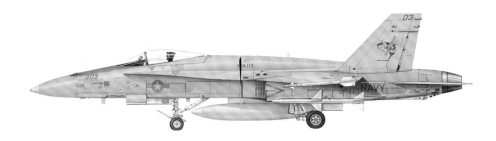

In the early 1970s, the US Navy had a requirement for a lightweight, inexpensive carrier-based aircraft that could be adapted for a variety of roles and used in conjunction with the more sophisticated and heavier Grumman F-14 Tomcat and as a replacement for the F-4 Phantom II and Vought A-7 Corsair II aircraft then in service. The USAF had a similar requirement to complement the F-15 Eagle, but opted for the rival F-16 Fighting Falcon. The Hornet was originally derived from the private venture Northrop YF-17. Northrop undertook development work in conjunction with McDonnell Douglas and are also involved in production. Although the aircraft was originally to have been produced in both fighter and attack versions, service aircraft are easily adapted to either role. Deliveries began in May 1980 to the US Navy and were completed in 1987.

SPECIFICATIONS

COUNTRY OF ORIGIN: United States

TYPE: single-seat fighter and strike aircraft

POWERPLANT: two 7264kg (16,000lb) General Electric F404-GE-400 turbofans

PERFORMANCE: maximum speed at 12,190m (40,000ft) 1912km/h (1183mph); combat ceiling 15,240m (50,000ft); combat radius 1065km (662 miles)

WEIGHT LOADED: empty 10,455kg (23,050lb); maximum take-off 25,401kg (56,000lb)

DIMENSIONS: wingspan 11.43m (37ft 6in); length 17.07m (56ft); height 4.66m (15ft 4in); wing area 37.16m² (400ft²)

ARMAMENT: one 20mm (0.79in) M61A1 Vulcan rotary cannon with 570 rounds; nine external hardpoints with provision for up to 7711kg (17,000kg) of stores, including air-to-air missiles, air-to-surface missiles, anti-ship missiles, free-fall or guided bombs, cluster bombs, dispenser weapons, napalm tanks, rocket launchers, drop tanks and ECM pods

McDonnell Douglas Phantom FG Mk1

The Royal Navy's decision to buy the Phantom was governed by a requirement that the aircraft be equipped with British built engines. To this end, an Anglicised version of the F-4J was produced, designated the F-4K, that was powered by two Rolls-Royce Spey turbofans. Fitting these engines necessitated widening the fuselage. Twenty-eight aircraft were delivered to the Navy from 1964, with a further 20 for the Royal Air Force. These aircraft are designated FG.Mk 1 in British use. The RAF also received a further 120 F-4M models, which incorporated the British features with those of the F-4C mentioned previously; these aircraft were designated FGR Mk 2 and also had the option to carry a centreline recce pod for tactical reconnaissance. The last aircraft in Royal Navy service was withdrawn in September 1978.

SPECIFICATIONS

COUNTRY OF ORIGIN: United States
TYPE: two-seat all-weather fighter/attack carrier-borne aircraft
POWERPLANT: two 9305kg (20,515lb) Rolls Royce Spey 202 turbofans
PERFORMANCE: maximum speed at high altitude 2230km/h (1386mph); service ceiling over 18,300m (60,000ft); range on internal fuel with no weapon load 2817km (1750 miles)
WEIGHT LOADED: empty 12,700kg (28,000lb); maximum take-off 26,308kg (58,000lb)
DIMENSIONS: span 11.7m (38ft 5in); length 17.55m (57ft 7in); height 4.96m (16ft 3in); wing area 49.24m² (530ft²)
ARMAMENT: four AIM-7 Sparrow recessed under fuselage; two wing pylons for two AIM-7, or four AIM-9 Sidewinder, provision for 20mm (0.79in) M61A1 cannon in external centreline pod; four wing pylons for tanks, bombs, or other stores to a maximum weight of 7257kg (16,000lb)

McDonnell Douglas RF-4C Phantom II

The importance of tactical reconnaissance was brought home to the USAF during the Korean war, and much emphasis was placed on this aspect of air operations in the following years. The exceptional performance of the Phantom II made it an ideal tool for reconnaissance work, leading to the development of the RF-4B. The aircraft were generally similar to the F-4B, but with lengthened nose to accommodate cameras, sideways-looking radar and infra-red sensors, which replaced the standard avionics equipment. Some 46 were built for the US Marine Corps with deliveries commencing in 1965. Confusingly, the USAF took delivery of 499 RF-4C aircraft (basically an F-4C airframe with the RF-4B equipment fit) from 1964. A reconnaissance version was also offered for export (RF-4E) in 1967 and was subsequently operated by Federal Germany, Greece, Turkey, Iran, Israel and Japan.

SPECIFICATIONS

COUNTRY OF ORIGIN: United States
TYPE: two-seat tactical reconnaissance aircraft
POWERPLANT: two 7711kg (17,000lb) General Electric J79-GE-8 turbojets
PERFORMANCE: maximum speed at 14,630m (48,000ft) 2390km/h (1485mph); service ceiling 18,900m (62,000ft); range 800km (500 miles)
WEIGHT LOADED: empty 13,768kg (30,328lb); maximum loaded 24,766kg (54,600lb)
DIMENSIONS: wingspan 11.7m (38ft 5in); length 18m (59ft); height 4.96m (16ft 3in); wing area 49.24m^2 (530ft^2)
ARMAMENT: none

McDonnell Douglas TA-4J Skyhawk

Few people believed Ed Heinemann – then chief designer at what was Douglas El Segundo – when he said he could build a jet attack bomber for the Navy at half of the 13,607kg (30,000lb) weight they specified. The first Skyhawk, nicknamed Heinemann's Hot Rod, gained a world record by flying a 500km circuit at over 695mph. The aircraft stayed in production for over 20 years, in a multiplicity of different versions. The TA-4J was a variant built for the US Navy, one of the main operators of the type. The fuselage is lengthened by approximately 0.76m (2.5ft) to accommodate the instructor in a tandem cockpit, reducing the internal fuel capacity. The tactical avionics suite is also reduced, and only one cannon is fitted. A version was also produced for the New Zealand air force, designated the TA-4K and also for the Kuwaiti air force (TA-4KU).

SPECIFICATIONS

COUNTRY OF ORIGIN: United States
TYPE: two-seat carrier trainer
POWERPLANT: one 3856kg (8500lb) J52-P-6 turbojet
PERFORMANCE: maximum speed 1084km/h (675mph); service ceiling 14,935m (49,000ft); range 1287km (800 miles)
WEIGHT LOADED: empty 4809kg (10,602lb); maximum take-off 11,113kg (24,500lb)
DIMENSIONS: wingspan 8.38m (27ft 6in); length excluding probe 12.98m (42ft 7in); height 4.66m (15ft 3in); wing area 24.15m^2 (260ft^2)
ARMAMENT: one 20mm (0.79in) cannon

Mikoyan-Gurevich MiG-15 'Fagot'

No aircraft in history has had a bigger impact on the world scene than the MiG-15. Its existence was unsuspected in the West until American fighter pilots found themselves confronted by all-swept silver fighters that could fly faster, climb and dive faster, and turn more tightly. The development of the aircraft could be traced back to the decision of the post-war British government to send to the Soviet Union the latest British turbojet, the Rolls Royce Nene, long before it was in service with any British service aircraft. This removed Mikoyan's problem of finding a suitable engine and, by the end of December 1947, the prototype was flying, powered by an unlicensed version of the Nene. Losses in Korea were high, mainly because of pilot inexperience, but as late as 1960 the Mig-15 was still used as a fighter by 15 countries.

SPECIFICATIONS

COUNTRY OF ORIGIN: Soviet Union
TYPE: single-seat fighter
POWERPLANT: one 2700kg (5952lb) Klimov VK-1 turbojet
PERFORMANCE: maximum speed 1100km/h (684 mph); service ceiling 15,545m (51,000ft); range at height with slipper tanks 1424km (885 miles)
WEIGHT LOADED: empty 4000kg (8820lb); maximum loaded 5700kg (12,566lb)
DIMENSIONS: wingspan 10.08m (33ft 1in); length 11.05m (36ft 3in); height 3.4m (11ft 2in); wing area 20.60m^2 (221.74ft^2)
ARMAMENT: one 37mm (1.46in) N-37 cannon and two 23mm (0.91in) NS-23 cannon, plus up to 500kg (1102lb) of mixed stores on underwing pylons

Mikoyan-Gurevich MiG-17F

Although outwardly similar to the MiG-15, the -17 was in fact a completely different aircraft. Western observers believed the aircraft had been hastily designed to rectify deficiencies shown in the MiG-15s performance during the Korean War, particularly the instability at speed which made it a difficult gun platform. In fact design of the -17 began in 1949, and was probably the last aircraft design in which Mikhail I. Gurevich had a direct personal role. The most important aspect of the new design was the wing, with the thickness reduced, a different section and platform and with three fences high speed behaviour was much improved. With a new tail on a longer rear fuselage, the transformation was completed by complete revision of the avionics fit. Service deliveries commenced in 1952 to the Soviet Air Force, with total production in excess of 5000.

SPECIFICATIONS

COUNTRY OF ORIGIN: Soviet Union
TYPE: single-seat fighter
POWERPLANT: one 3383kg (7,452lb) Klimov VK-1F turbojet
PERFORMANCE: maximum speed at 3000m (9840ft) 1145km/h (711mph); service ceiling 16,600m (54,560ft); range at height with slipper tanks 1470km (913 miles)
WEIGHT LOADED: empty 4100kg (9040lb); maximum loaded 6,00kg (14,770lb)
DIMENSIONS: wingspan 9.45m (31ft); length 11.05m (36ft 3in); height 3.35m (11ft); wing area 20.60m^2 (221.74ft^2)
ARMAMENT: one 37mm (1.46in) N-37 cannon and two 23mm (0.91in) NS-23 cannon, plus up to 500kg (1102lb) of mixed stores on underwing pylons

Mikoyan-Gurevich MiG-19PM

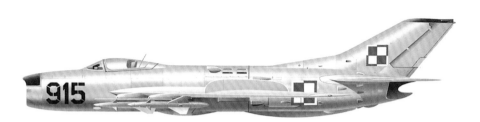

With the unveiling of the Mig-19 the Mikoyan-Gurevich bureau established itself at the forefront of the world's fighter design teams. The new fighter was in the preliminary design stage before the Mig-15 had been encountered over Korea, with five prototypes ordered in July 1951. The first flew in September 1953, powered by twin AM-5 engines. With afterburning engines the MiG-19 became the first supersonic engines in Soviet service. Steadily improved versions culminated in the MiG-19PM, with guns removed and pylons for four early beamrider air-to-air missiles. In 1960 this simple, extremely potent aircraft was judged obsolete by Western observers. By 1970 the performance of Chinese-built F-6 (MiG-19SF) in North Vietnamese and Pakistani service led to it being reappraised by NATO. In the late 1990s some aircraft remained in service with training units.

SPECIFICATIONS

COUNTRY OF ORIGIN: Italy
TYPE: single-seat all-weather interceptor
POWERPLANT: two 3250kg (7165lb) Klimov RD-9B turbojets
PERFORMANCE: maximum speed at 9080m (20,000ft) 1480km/h (920mph); service ceiling 17,900m (58,725ft); maximum range at high altitude with two drop tanks 2200km (1367 miles)
WEIGHT LOADED: empty 5760kg (12,698lb); maximum take-off 9500kg (20,944lb)
DIMENSIONS: wingspan 9m (29ft 6in); length 13.58m (44ft 7in); height 4.02m (13ft 2in); wing area 25m^2 (269.11ft^2)
ARMAMENT: underwing pylons for four AA-1 Alkali air-to-air-missiles, or AA-2 Atoll

Mikoyan-Gurevich MiG-21bis

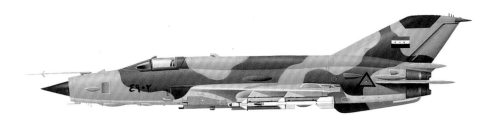

The MiG-21 established a reputation as one of the most versatile combat aircraft of the post-war era. With production totalling a figure estimated at more than 11,000, the 'Fishbed' has served with 39 air forces. The aircraft was developed in 18 months following the Korean War. At least 30 pre-production aircraft were manufactured, before service deliveries of the MiG-21F 'Fishbed-C' began in 1958. The MiG-21bis 'Fishbed-N' pictured here was an improved version of the MiG-21bis 'Fishbed-L', which first appeared in 1971, and introduced new advanced construction techniques, greater fuel capacity and updated avionics for multi role air combat and ground attack. In 1975 the 'Fishbed-N' was introduced and, in addition to these improvements, the 'N' had more powerful turbojets and further uprated avionics.

SPECIFICATIONS

COUNTRY OF ORIGIN: Soviet Union
TYPE: single-seat all-weather multi role fighter
POWERPLANT: one 7507kg (16,535lb) Tumanskii R-25 turbojets
PERFORMANCE: maximum speed above 11,000m (36,090ft) 2229km/h (1385mph); service ceiling 17,500m (57,400ft); range on internal fuel 1160km (721 miles)
WEIGHT LOADED: empty 5200kg (11,464lb); maximum take-off 10,400kg (22,925lb)
DIMENSIONS: wingspan 7.15m (23ft 6in); length (including probe) 15.76m (51ft 9in); height 4.10m (13ft 6in); wing area 23m^2 (247.58ft^2)
ARMAMENT: one 23mm (0.91in) GSh-23 twin-barrell cannon in underbelly pack, four underwing pylons with provision for about 1500kg (3307kg) of stores, including AA-2 Atoll or AA-8 Aphid air-to-air missiles, UV-16-57 rocket pods, napalm tanks, or drop tanks

Mikoyan-Gurevich MiG-21U

The two seat trainer version of the MiG-21F was known in the West by the NATO designated name 'Mongol'. Aside from the airframe modifications necessary to accommodate the instructor, the -21U is similar in configuration to the initial major production version, the -21F. The first prototype is reported to have flown in 1960. Variations from the single-seater include a one-piece forward airbrake, deletion of the cannon armament, repositioning of the pilot boom, adoption of larger mainwheels first introduced on the MiG-21PF. Further revisions were adopted on the -21US and -21UM models. These included vertical tail surfaces of revised design and a deeper dorsal spine. The aircraft is still used widely throughout in former Eastern Bloc countries and in India, where it was built under licence by HAL. This is one of the aircraft operated by the Finnish air force.

SPECIFICATIONS

COUNTRY OF ORIGIN: Soviet Union
TYPE: two-seat trainer
POWERPLANT: one 5950kg (13,118lb) Tumanskii R-11F2S-300 turbojet
PERFORMANCE: maximum speed above 12,200m (40,025ft) 2145km/h (1333mph); service ceiling 17,500m (57,400ft); range on internal fuel 1160km (721 miles)
WEIGHT LOADED: not released
DIMENSIONS: wingspan 7.15m (23ft 6in); length (including probe) 15.76m (51ft 9in); height 4.10m (13ft 6in); wing area 23m^2 (247.58ft^2)
ARMAMENT: none

Mikoyan-Gurevich MiG-23M

By 1975 several hundred MiG-23s, including the attack and trainer versions, had been delivered to Warsaw Pact air forces. Production continued until the mid-1980s; by far the largest operator was the Soviet Union. It was reported during the late-1980s that the US had acquired former Egyptian operated MiG-23s for realistic air-to-air combat training of USAF and NATO pilots. Soviet operated aircraft differ from export models by having the Sapfir-23D-Sh 'High Lark' fire-control radar, and infra-red search/track system and pulse Doppler navigation. These aircraft are numerically still the most important Russian interceptors, though the fleet as a whole is in a poor state due to shortages of funding. The engine – one of the most powerful to be fitted to a combat aircraft – gives good short field performance and high top speed.

SPECIFICATIONS

COUNTRY OF ORIGIN: Soviet Union
TYPE: single-seat air combat fighter
POWERPLANT: one 10,208kg (22,485lb) Khachaturov R-29-300 turbojet
PERFORMANCE: maximum speed at altitude about 2445km/h (1520mph); service ceiling over 18,290m (60,000ft); combat radius on hi-lo-hi mission 966km (600 miles)
WEIGHT LOADED: empty 10,400kg (22,932lb); maximum loaded 18,145kg (40,000lb)
DIMENSIONS: wingspan 13.97m (45ft 10in) spread and 7.78m (25ft 6in) swept; length (including probe) 16.71m (54ft 10in); height 4.82m (15ft 10in); wing area 37.25m^2 (402ft^2) spread
ARMAMENT: one 23mm (0.91in) GSh-23L cannon, underwing pylons for AA-3 Anab, AA-7 Apex, and/or AA-8 Aphid air-to-air missiles

Mikoyan-Gurevich MiG-23MF

Although undoubtedly a fine aircraft, the MiG-21 was hampered by limited payload/range performance. In 1965 a requirement was issued for a replacement to help try and rectify these problems. Mikoyan-Gurevich submitted two proposals, one for an enlarged version of the MiG-21, and an alternative which was later realised as the Ye-23-11/1 prototype. The aircraft formed the basis for the MiG-23 and was first publicly displayed at the 1967 Aviation Day flypast. Apart from the variable geometry wing, the other major variation on early MiG jet aircraft were side inlets to allow incorporation of search radar and allow for greater internal fuel capacity. The MiG-23M 'Flogger-B' was the first series production version, and entered service in 1972 with the Soviet Union and later Warsaw pact air forces.

SPECIFICATIONS

COUNTRY OF ORIGIN: Soviet Union

TYPE: single-seat air combat fighter

POWERPLANT: one 10,208kg (22,485lb) Khachaturov R-29-300 turbojet

PERFORMANCE: maximum speed at altitude about 2445km/h (1520mph); service ceiling over 18,290m (60,000ft); combat radius on hi-lo-hi mission 966km (600 miles)

WEIGHT LOADED: empty 10,400kg (22,932lb); maximum loaded 18,145kg (40,000lb)

DIMENSIONS: wingspan 13.97m (45ft 10in) spread and 7.78m (25ft 6in) swept; length (including probe) 16.71m (54ft 10in); height 4.82m (15ft 10in); wing area 37.25m^2 (402ft^2)spread

ARMAMENT: one 23mm (0.91in) GSh-23L cannon, underwing pylons for AA-3 Anab, AA-7 Apex, and/or AA-8 Aphid air-to-air missiles

Mikoyan-Gurevich MiG-23UB

Atwo-seat version of the MiG-23 was produced for conversion training, powered by the Tumanskii R-27 turbojet and equipped with the 'Jay Bird' radar of export. The second cockpit – for the instructor – is to the rear of the standard cockpit. The seat is slightly raised and is provided with a retractable periscopic sight to give a more comprehensive forward view. Like most Soviet military aircraft produced during the Cold War, it retains full combat capability and has the NATO reporting name MiG-23UB 'Flogger-C'. Libya was one of the first countries to take delivery of the aircraft, which is also in service with several other Arab nations. Though these nations have taken delivery of what are advanced combat aircraft, pilot training and servicing provision on the ground remains poor, thus affecting overall effectiveness.

SPECIFICATIONS

COUNTRY OF ORIGIN: Soviet Union
TYPE: two-seat conversion trainer
POWERPLANT: one Tumanskii 10,000kg (22,046lb) R-27F2M-300 turbojet
PERFORMANCE: maximum speed at altitude about 2445km/h (1520mph); service ceiling over 18,290m (60,000ft); operational radius about 966km (600 miles)
WEIGHT LOADED: empty 11,000kg (24,200lb); maximum loaded 18,145kg (40,000lb)
DIMENSIONS: wingspan 13.97m (45ft 10in) spread and 7.78m (25ft 6in) swept; length (including probe) 16.71m (54ft 10in); height 4.82m (15ft 10in); wing area 37.25m^2 (402ft^2) spread
ARMAMENT: one 23mm (0.91in) GSh-23L cannon with 200 rounds; six external hardpoints with provision for up to 3000kg (6614lb) of stores, including air-to-air missiles, cannon pods, rocket-launcher pods, and bombs

Mikoyan-Gurevich MiG-25P

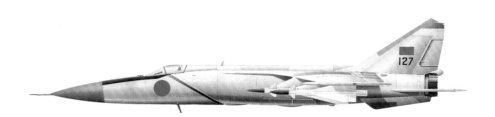

Reports of the development of a long-range high speed strategic bomber in the US in the late 1950s – the B-70 Valkyrie – prompted the Soviet authorities to give highest priority to the design and development of an interceptor that could be operational to meet the B-70s planned 1964 in-service date. Even when the B-70 programme was cancelled in 1961, work continued on the development of the interceptor known as the MiG-25 and was given the NATO reporting name 'Foxbat'. The aircraft was unveiled publicly at the 1967 Moscow Aviation Day. The prototypes blazed a trail of world records in 1965–67, and when the MiG-25P production aircraft entered service in 1970 it far outclassed any Western aircraft in terms of speed and height. This aircraft is also operated by Libya, Algeria, India, Iraq and Syria.

SPECIFICATIONS

COUNTRY OF ORIGIN: Soviet Union
TYPE: single-seat interceptor
POWERPLANT: two 10,200kg (22,487lb) Tumanskii R-15B-300 turbojets
PERFORMANCE: maximum speed at altitude about 2974km/h (1848mph); service ceiling over 24,385m (80,000ft); combat radius 1130km (702 miles)
WEIGHT LOADED: empty 20,000kg (44,092lb); maximum take-off 37,425kg (82,508lb)
DIMENSIONS: wingspan 14.02m (46ft); length 23.82m (78ft 2in); height 6.10m (20ft); wing area 61.40m^2 (660.9ft^2)
ARMAMENT: external pylons for four air-to-air missiles in the form of either two each of the IR- and radar-homing AA-6 'Acrid', or two AA-7 'Apex' and two AA-8 'Aphid' weapons

Mikoyan-Gurevich MiG-29

In 1972 the Soviet Air Force began seeking a replacement for the MiG-21, -23, Sukhoi Su-15, and -17 fleets then in service. The MiG bureau submitted the winning entry and flight testing of the new fighter, designated 'Ram L' (later 'Fulcrum') by Western intelligence, began in October 1977. First deliveries of the aircraft were made to Soviet Frontal Aviation units in 1983 and the type became operational in 1985. A more detailed analysis of the aircraft was not possible until 1986, when a detachment of the aircraft visited Finland. The visit confirmed many estimates as to the size and configuration of the aircraft. More than 600 of the first production model, the 'Fulcrum-A', were delivered, with two important export orders to Syria and India. Deliveries to No. 28 Squadron and No. 47 Squadron of the Indian air force began in 1986.

SPECIFICATIONS

COUNTRY OF ORIGIN: Soviet Union
TYPE: single-seat air-superiority fighter with secondary ground attack capability
POWERPLANT: two 8300kg (18,298lb) Sarkisov RD-33 turbofans
PERFORMANCE: maximum speed above 11,000m (36,090ft) 2443km/h (1518mph); service ceiling 17,000m (55,775ft); range with internal fuel 1500km (932 miles)
WEIGHT LOADED: empty 10,900kg (24,030lb); maximum take-off 18,500kg (40,785lb)
DIMENSIONS: wingspan 11.36m (37ft 3in); length (including probe) 17.32m (56ft 10in); height 7.78m (25ft 6in); wing area 35.2m^2 (378.9ft^2)
ARMAMENT: one 30mm (1.18in) GSh-30 cannon with 150 rounds, eight external hardpoints with provision for up to 4500kg (9921lb) of stores, including six AA-11 'Archer' and AA-10 'Alamo' infra-red or radar guided air-to-air missiles, rocket launcher pods, large calibre rockets, napalm tanks, drop tanks, ECM pods, conventional and guided bombs

Mikoyan-Gurevich MiG-29M

Work commenced on advanced versions of the MiG-29 at the end of the 1970s, with work concentrated on improving the range and versatility of the aircraft. One of the most significant changes was the incorporation of an advanced analog fly-by-wire control system, coupled with improved Head-Up and Head-Down displays. Physical appearance is similar, although the MiG-29M has an extended chord tailplane, and a recontoured dorsal fairing. Other changes are a more reliable and fuel efficient version of the Sarkisov turbofans, updated avionics with an advanced radar data processor four times the power of its predecessor, rearward shift in the centre of gravity to complement the fly-by-wire system, and two extra underwing hardpoints. These improvements all make for a better aircraft, but despite its potential it has not been ordered by the Russian air force.

SPECIFICATIONS

COUNTRY OF ORIGIN: Soviet Union
TYPE: single-seat air-superiority fighter with secondary ground attack capability
POWERPLANT: two 9,409kg (20,725lb) Sarkisov RD-33K turbofans
PERFORMANCE: maximum speed above 11000m (36,090ft) 2300km/h (1430mph); service ceiling 17,000m (55,775ft); range with internal fuel 1500km (932 miles)
WEIGHT LOADED: empty 10,900kg (24,030lb); maximum take-off 18,500kg (40,785lb)
DIMENSIONS: wingspan 11.36m (37ft 3in); length (including probe) 17.32m (56ft 10in); height 7.78m (25ft 6in); wing area 35.2m^2 (378.9ft^2)
ARMAMENT: one 30mm (1.18in) GSh-30 cannon with 150 rounds, six external hardpoints with provision for up to 3000kg (6614lb) of stores, including six AA-11 'Archer' and AA-10 'Alamo' infra-red or radar guided air-to-air missiles, rocket launcher pods, large calibre rockets, napalm tanks, drop tanks, ECM pods, conventional and guided bombs

Mikoyan-Gurevich MiG-31

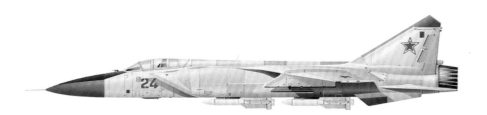

The MiG-31 was developed during the 1970s from the impressive MiG-25 'Foxbat' to counter the threat from low-flying cruise missiles and bombers. A prototype first flew in September 1975, but it gradually became clear that the new aircraft was far more than a new-generation 'Foxbat'. In fact the MiG-31 was a vast improvement over its older stablemate, with tandem seat cockpit, IR search and tracking sensor, and the Zaslon 'Flash Dance' pulse-Doppler radar providing genuine fire-and-forget engagement capability against multiple targets flying at lower altitudes. The 'Foxhound-A' entered service in 1983 with the Voyska PVO. The aircraft pictured wears the colours of the former Soviet air force, based in the Arkhangel'sk district. Further development of the aircraft has been hampered by cut-backs in defence expenditure.

SPECIFICATIONS

COUNTRY OF ORIGIN: Soviet Union
TYPE: two-seat all weather interceptor and ECM aircraft
POWERPLANT: two 15,500kg (34,171lb) Soloviev D-30F6 turbofans
PERFORMANCE: maximum speed at 17,500m (57,400ft) 3000km/h (1865mph); service ceiling 20,600m (67,600ft); combat radius with four AAMs and two drop tanks 1400km (840 miles)
WEIGHT LOADED: empty 21,825kg (48,415lb); maximum take-off 46,200kg (101,850lb)
DIMENSIONS: wingspan 13.46m (44ft 2in); length 22.68m (74ft 5in); height 6.15m (20ft 2in); wing area 61.6m² (663ft²)
ARMAMENT: one 23mm (0.91in) GSh-23-6 cannon with 260 rounds, eight external hardpoints with provision for four AA-9 'Amos' and two AA-6 'Acrid' or four AA-8 'Aphid' air-to-air missiles, ECM pods, or drop tanks

Mikoyan-Gurevich MiG-35

The MiG-35, given the NATO reporting name 'Fulcrum-F', is the latest member of a family of multirole combat aircraft. It is significantly more advanced and capable than previous version, and uses a Western-standard electronics bus. This allows the Fulcrum-F to use weaponry from a range of manufacturers in addition to Russian systems. Cockpit avionics make extensive use of multifunction displays, enabling the pilot to reconfigure his displays at need. In a modern multirole aircraft that might switch missions in flight, this capability is extremely useful. The MiG-35 mounts a 30mm (1.18in) cannon and can carry a range of ordnance on nine external hardpoints, including advanced air-to-air missiles and precision guided weapons. Reliability has also been improved compared to earlier incarnations of the Fulcrum family. The MiG-35 was designed with the export market in mind, and has attracted international interest, notably from India.

SPECIFICATIONS

COUNTRY OF ORIGIN: Russia

TYPE: single or two-seat twin-engined multirole combat aircraft

POWERPLANT: two Klimov RD-33MK afterburning turbofans delivering 53kN (11,900lb) thrust per engine

PERFORMANCE: Mach 2.5; 2400km/h (1491mph) at altitude; initial climb: 330m/s (65,000ft/min); ceiling: 17,500m (57,400ft); range: 2000km (1242.2 miles)

WEIGHT LOADED: empty: 11,000kg (24,250.85lbs); maximum takeoff: 29,700kg (65,477.29lbs)

DIMENSIONS: 15m (49ft 3in); length: 19m (62ft 4in); height 6m (19ft 8in)

ARMAMENT: one GSh-30-1 30mm (1.18in) cannon; 6500kg (14,330lbs) of additional ordnance including guided and unguided bombs, missiles, rockets and external fuel tanks

Mitsubishi T-2

To replace the T-1 tandem-seat trainer (Japan's first post-war military aircraft) a team led by Dr Kenji Ikeda designed the T-2, using the Anglo-French SEPECAT Jaguar as a basis. After flight trials had proved the validity of the design a singleseat version, the FST-2-Kai was ordered (see F-1). The two aircraft are almost identical apart from the rear cockpit and addition of tubular passive warning radar aerial along the top of the fin. By mid-1975, orders had been placed for the T-2, powered by Ishikawajima-Harima built versions of the Rolls Royce Turbomeca Adour turbofans. The aircraft entered service in 1976 with the 4th Air Wing at Mitsushima; its success in operational service has underlined the benefits of commonality with the F-1 fighter. This aircraft wears the colours of the 'Blue Impulse' aerobatic team of the JASDF, a component of the 4th Kokudan.

SPECIFICATIONS

COUNTRY OF ORIGIN: Japan
TYPE: two-seat advanced flying, weapon and combat trainer
POWERPLANT: two 3315kg (7308lb) Ishikawajima-Harima TF40-IHI-801A turbofans
PERFORMANCE: maximum speed at 10,675m (35,000ft) 1708km/h (1061mph); service ceiling 15,240m (50,000ft); combat radius on hi-lo-hi mission with 1816kg (4000lb) load 350km (218 miles)
WEIGHT LOADED: empty 6307kg (13,904lb); maximum take-off 12,800kg (28,219lb)
DIMENSIONS: wingspan 7.88m (25ft 10in); length 17.86m (58ft 7in); height 4.39m (14ft 5in); wing area 21.17m² (227.88ft²)
ARMAMENT: one 20mm (0.79in) JM61Vulcan six-barrell cannon with 750 rounds, five external hardpoints with provision for 2722kg (6000lb) of stores, including air-to-surface missiles, conventional and guided bombs, rocket-launcher pods, drop tanks, ECM pods; two wingtip pylons for air-to-air missiles

Morane-Saulnier MS.760 Paris

The MS.760 is the more successful four-seater version of the MS.755 Fleuret, which made an unsuccessful bid to win the early 1950s Armée de l'Air competition for a jet trainer. The Morane-Saulnier company, which later became part of Potez in 1963, proceeded with development of the low-wing cabin monoplane and the first prototype flew in July 1954. Orders were received from both the Armée de l'Air and the Aéronavale as well as a number of overseas clients, including Brazil and Argentina. In 1961 production switched to the MS.760B Paris II, with more powerful engines, leading edge fuel tanks and improved baggage space. A total of 165 Paris Is and IIs were completed before production ended in 1964. A handful still serve as liaison aircraft with the Aéronavale and Argentina.

SPECIFICATIONS

COUNTRY OF ORIGIN: France
TYPE: four/five-seat liason and light transport aircraft
POWERPLANT: two 400kg (882lb) Turbomeca Marbore turbojets
PERFORMANCE: maximum speed at 7620m (25,000ft) 695km/h (432mph); service ceiling 12,000m (39,370ft); range 1740km (1081 miles)
WEIGHT LOADED: empty 2067kg (4557lb); maximum take-off 3920kg (8642lb)
DIMENSIONS: wingspan 10.15m (33ft 4in); length 10.24m (33ft 7in); height 2.6m (8ft 7in); wing area 18m^2 (193.76ft^2)
ARMAMENT: none in liason/transport role; Argentina have used theirs in COIN role with two 7.62mm (0.3in) machine guns in nose, and two 50kg (110lb) bombs or four 90mm (3.54in) rockets under wings

North American F-86D Sabre

One of the most famous combat aircraft of the post war era, the Sabre was developed to meet a US Army Air Force requirement for a day fighter that could also be used as an escort fighter or dive-bomber. The F-86D was designed as an all-weather interceptor, and although development did not commence until 1949, the first prototype flew from Muroc Dry Lake on 22 December of that year. The F-86D was highly complex for its time, and introduced the new concept of gunless collision-course interception directed by a AN/APG-36 search radar above the nose intake and an autopilot. This was the most extensively built of all the Sabre series, with 2054 completed. At the peak of its deployment in the 1950s some 20 Air Defence Command wings were equipped with the type. This aircraft was supplied to many NATO countries under the Military Aid Program.

SPECIFICATIONS

COUNTRY OF ORIGIN: United States
TYPE: single-seat all-weather/night interceptor
POWERPLANT: one 3402kg (7500lb) General Electric J47-GE-17B or -33 turbojet
PERFORMANCE: maximum speed at sea level 1138km/h (707mph); service ceiling 16,640m (54,600ft); range 1344km (835 miles)
WEIGHT LOADED: empty 5656kg (12,470lb); maximum take-off 7756kg (17,100lb)
DIMENSIONS: wingspan 11.30m (37ft 1in); length 12.29m (40ft 4in); height 4.57m (15ft); wing area 27.76m^2 (288ft^2)
ARMAMENT: 24 69.85mm (2.75in) 'Mighty Mouse' air-to-air rocket projectiles in retractable tray under cockpit floor

North American F-86F Sabre

The F-86F Sabre was basically an uprated version of the F-84E, which had introduced the powered all-flying tailplane and slatted wing. The F-86F had further refinements, such as an extended leading edge, increased chord and a small wing fence. Both aircraft saw extensive service in the Vietnam conflict. The first Sabre units in Korea were equipped with the earlier 'A' model; the 'F' began to arrive in theatre with the 8th and 18th Fighter Bomber Wings in early 1953. The aircraft was flown brilliantly against the MiG-15. Despite having marginally inferior performance to the Russian aircraft, the disparity was more than matched by the superior training and experience of American pilots. Total production of the F-86F totalled 1079; from 1954, many were delivered to America's allies under the Military Aid Program.

SPECIFICATIONS

COUNTRY OF ORIGIN: United States
TYPE: single-seat fighter-bomber
POWERPLANT: one 2710kg (5970lb) General Electric J47-GE-27turbojet
PERFORMANCE: maximum speed at sea level 1091km/h (678mph); service ceiling 15,240m (50,000ft); range 1344km (835 miles)
WEIGHT LOADED: empty 5045kg (11,125lb); maximum loaded 9350kg (20,611lb)
DIMENSIONS: wingspan 11.30m (37ft 1in); length 11.43m (37ft 6in); height 4.47m (14ft 8in); wing area 27.76m^2 (288ft^2)
ARMAMENT: six 0.5 Colt-Browning M-3 with 267 rpg, underwing hardpoints for two tanks or two stores of 454kg (1000lb), plus eight rockets

North American F-100D Super Sabre

The resounding success of the Sabre made it only natural that North American would attempt to build a successor. This was planned from 1949 as a larger and more powerful machine able to exceed *the spe*ed of sound in level flight. After a very rapid development programme and with the first (479th) wing operational, the F-100A was grounded in November 1954 due to stability problems. After modifications to the wings and fin, the F-100 enjoyed a trouble-free and successful career. The 203A fighter versions produced were followed by structurally strengthened C fighter-bombers, a flap and autopilot equipped D variant and a tandem seat F model. Total production was 2294, with many aircraft serving in Vietnam. The F-100D was an improved version with larger fin and rudder, increased external stores capacity, and for the first time, landing flaps.

SPECIFICATIONS

COUNTRY OF ORIGIN: United States
TYPE: single-seat fighter-bomber
POWERPLANT: one 7711kg (17,000lb) Pratt & Whitney J57-P-21A turbojet
PERFORMANCE: maximum speed at 10,670m (35,000ft) 1390km/h (864mph); service ceiling 14,020m (46,000ft); range with inernal fuel 966km (600 miles)
WEIGHT LOADED: empty 9525kg (21,000lb); maximum take-off 15,800kg (34,832lb)
DIMENSIONS: wingspan 11.82m (38ft 9in); length excluding probe 14.36m (47ft 1in); height 4.95m (16ft 3in); wing area 35.77m^2 (385ft^2)
ARMAMENT: four 20mm (0.79in) cannon; eight external hardpoints with provision for two drop tanks and up to 3402kg (7500lb) of stores, bombs, cluster bombs, dispenser weapons, rocket-launcher pods, cannon pods, and ECM pods

North American FJ-1 Fury

The FJ-1 Fury was one of three jet-powered aircraft ordered for evaluation purposes by the US Navy. The three prototypes were heavily influenced by German wartime research; the North American NA-134, which was to become the FJ-1 Fury, flew in November 1946. One hundred production aircraft had been ordered in May 1945, but this was subsequently cut to 30. Production deliveries began in March 1948 to Naval Squadron VF-5A, who made the first carrier landings with the aircraft on the tenth day of that month on USS *Boxer*. Although it had a relatively undistinguished career, the Fury was the first aircraft to complete an operational tour at sea, and paved the way for the more aesthetically pleasing F-86 Sabre. For a brief period it could also claim to be the fastest aircraft in US Navy service.

SPECIFICATIONS

COUNTRY OF ORIGIN: United States
TYPE: single-seat carrier-borne fighter
POWERPLANT: one 1816kg (4000lb) Allison J35-A-2 turbojet
PERFORMANCE: maximum speed at 2743m (9000ft) 880km/h (547mph); service ceiling 9754m (32,000ft); range 2414km (1500 miles)
WEIGHT LOADED: empty 4011kg (8843lb); maximum loaded 7076kg (15,600lb)
DIMENSIONS: wingspan 9.8m (38ft 2in); length 10.5m (34ft 5in); height 4.5m (14ft 10in); wing area 20.5m^2 (221ft^2)
ARMAMENT: six 12.7mm (0.5in) machine guns

North American FJ-3M Fury

Both Army and Navy contracts were awarded to North American in 1944 for a jet fighter, but the land-based programme moved fastest. After the land-based program had discarded the straight-wing configuration of the early design for an all-swept format, the naval team persisted with it and produced the unremarkable FJ-1 Fury. Before this aircraft had even entered service, the US Navy was seeking its replacement. This aircraft, the FJ-2, was in essence a navalized version of the company's land-based F-86E Sabre, with folding wings, strengthened landing gear and catapult hitches, and arrestor gear. Some 200 were produced and served with the US Marines. They were superseded by the FJ-3, which had a larger, more powerful engine, which necessitated increasing the depth of the fuselage, a new canopy, extended leading edge, and increased weapon load.

SPECIFICATIONS

COUNTRY OF ORIGIN: United States
TYPE: single-seat fighter-bomber
POWERPLANT: one 3648kg (7800lb) Wright J65-W-2 turbojet
PERFORMANCE: maximum speed at sea level 1091km/h (678mph); service ceiling 16,640m (54,600ft); range 1344km (835 miles)
WEIGHT LOADED: empty 5051kg (11,125lb); maximum loaded 9350kg (20,611lb)
DIMENSIONS: wingspan 11.30m (37ft 1in); length 11.43m (37ft 6in); height 4.47m (14ft 8in); wing area 27.76m² (288ft²)
ARMAMENT: six 12.7mm (0.5in) Colt-Browning M-3 with 267rpg, underwing hardpoints for two tanks or two stores of 454kg (1000lb), plus eight rockets

Northrop CF-5A

In partnership with the Netherlands, the Canadair company licence built versions of the single-seat F-5A and two-seat F-5B for the Canadian Armed Forces, and Netherlands air force. The Canadian aircraft are designated CF-5A/CF-5D. In 1987, Bristol Aerospace Ltd of Winnipeg received a contract to upgrade and extend the service life of 56 CF-5A and -D aircraft and optimize them for lead-in training for CF-18 Hornets. This program involved reskinning the wings and vertical stabilizer, reinforcement of various fuselage parts and replacement of the landing gear. With airframe life extended by another 4000 hours, installation of advance avionics and incorporation of aerodynamic improvements, the Bristol re-furbished F-5A/B becomes the F5-2000, indicating continuation of service beyond the year 2000. Cost of the first modified aircraft, returned to service in 1991, was quoted as $4 million.

SPECIFICATIONS

COUNTRY OF ORIGIN: United States
TYPE: light tactical fighter
POWERPLANT: two 1950kg (4300lb) Orenda (General Electric) J85-CAN-13 turbojets
PERFORMANCE: maximum speed at 10,975m (36,000ft) 1487km/h (924mph); service ceiling 15,390m (50,500ft); combat radius with maximum warload 314km (195 miles)
WEIGHT LOADED: empty 3667kg (8085lb); maximum take-off 9374kg (20,667lb)
DIMENSIONS: wingspan 7.7m (25ft 3in); length 14.38m (47ft 2in); height 4.01m (13ft 2in); wing area 15.79m^2 (170ft^2)
ARMAMENT: two 20mm (0.79in) M39 cannon with 280rpg; provision for 1996kg (4400lb) of stores on external pylons, (including two air-to-air missiles on wingtip pylons), bombs, cluster bombs, rocket launcher pods

Northrop F-5A Freedom Fighter

In 1955, Northrop began the design of a lightweight fighter powered by two underslung J85 missile engines. This was yet another of the countless projects born during the Korean era when pilots were calling for lighter, simpler fighters with higher performance. The design team led by Welko Gasich refined the design, putting the engines in the fuselage and increasing their size. From this aircraft, the T-38 Talon, was developed the F-5A, which was largely a privately funded project by Northrop. In October 1962, the US Department of Defense decided to buy the aircraft in large numbers to supply to friendly countries on advantageous terms. More than 1000 were supplied to Iran, Taiwan, Greece, South Korea, Phillipines, Turkey, Ethiopia, Morocco, Norway, Thailand, Libya, and South Vietnam. The aircraft pictured is an F-5A of the 341 Mira, Hellenic (Greek) air force.

SPECIFICATIONS

COUNTRY OF ORIGIN: United States
TYPE: light tactical fighter
POWERPLANT: two 1850kg (4080lb) General Electric J85-GE-13 turbojets
PERFORMANCE: maximum speed at 10,975m (36,000ft) 1487km/h (924mph); service ceiling 15,390m (50,500ft); combat radius with maximum warload 314km (195 miles)
WEIGHT LOADED: empty 3667kg (8085lb); maximum take-off 9374kg (20,667lb)
DIMENSIONS: wingspan 7.7m (25ft 3in); length 14.38m (47ft 2in); height 4.01m (13ft 2in); wing area 15.79m^2 (170ft^2)
ARMAMENT: two 20mm (0.79in) M39 cannon with 280rpg; provision for 1996kg (4400lb) of stores on external pylons, (including two air-to-air missiles on wingtip pylons), bombs, cluster bombs, rocket launcher pods

Northrop F-5E Tiger II

The F-5E Tiger II won a US industry competition in November 1970 for a followon International Fighter Aircraft to replace the F-5A. The improved aircraft is equipped with more powerful powerplants, extending nosegear to improve short field performance, extra fuel in a longer fuselage, new inlet ducts, widened fuselage and wing, root extensions ad manoeuvring flaps. Deliveries began in 1972. The US Air Force operates the aircraft for aggressor training in the US, UK and the Philippines. The aircraft pictured is operated by the US Navy's Fighter Weapons School at Naval Air Station Miramar in California. The manouevrability of the F-5 makes it a formidable opponent in air combat training. A two-seat trainer version is also produced with designation F-JF. Both aircraft retain full combat capability. The F-5E has also been supplied to the Royal Saudi Air Force.

SPECIFICATIONS

COUNTRY OF ORIGIN: United States
TYPE: light tactical fighter
POWERPLANT: two 2268kg (5000lb) General Electric J85-GE-21B turbojets
PERFORMANCE: maximum speed at 10,975m (36,000ft) 1741km/h (1082mph); service ceiling 15,790m (51,800ft); combat radius with maximum warload 306km (190 miles)
WEIGHT LOADED: empty 4410kg (9723lb); maximum take-off 11,214kg (24,722lb)
DIMENSIONS: wingspan 8.13m (26ft 8in); length 14.45m (47ft 5in); height 4.07m (13ft 4in); wing area 17.28m^2 (186ft^2)
ARMAMENT: two 20mm (0.79in) M39 cannon with 280 rpg; two air-to-air missiles on wingtip pylons, five external pylons with provision for 3175kg (7000lb) of stores, including air-to-surface missiles, bombs, cluster bombs, rocket launcher pods, ECM pods, and drop tanks

Northrop RF-5E TigerEye

The RF-5E is a reconnaissance version of the F-5E Tiger, the improved version of the Freedom Fighter detailed elsewhere. The export success of this aircraft led to the development of a specialised tactical reconnaissance version, which first appeared at the Paris Air Show in 1978. Externally, the RF-5E is similar to the fighter, except for an extended 'chisel' nose housing camera equipment and refuelling probe. Internally, the aircraft can carry a wide range of reconnaissance equipment, on easily interchangeable pallets. The pilot also has the benefit of advanced navigation and communications systems, to allow him to concentrate on operation of the reconnaissance equipment. The aircraft pictured is operated by the Royal Saudi Air Force. Saudi and Malaysia were the only two countries to buy the aircraft.

SPECIFICATIONS

COUNTRY OF ORIGIN: United States
TYPE: light tactical reconnaissance fighter
POWERPLANT: two 2268kg (5000lb) General Electric J85-GE-21B turbojets
PERFORMANCE: maximum speed at 10,975m (36,000ft) 1741km/h (1082mph); service ceiling 15,390m (50,500ft); combat radius on internal fuel 463km (288 miles)
WEIGHT LOADED: empty 4423kg (9750lb); maximum take-off 11,192kg (24,765lb)
DIMENSIONS: wingspan 8.13m (26ft 8in); length 14.65m (48ft 1in); height 4.07m (13ft 4in); wing area 17.28m^2 (186ft^2)
ARMAMENT: one 20mm (0.79in) M39 cannon with 140 rounds; two air-to-air missiles on wingtip pylons, five external pylons with provision for 3175kg (7000lb) of stores, including air-to-surface missiles, bombs, cluster bombs, rocket launcher pods, ECM pods, and drop tanks

Northrop T-38A Talon

The T-38A trainer aircraft was derived from a requirement issued by the US government in the mid-1950s for a lightweight fighter to supply to friendly nations under the Military Assistance Program. The initial privately funded Northrop design formed the basis for a family of aircraft which also included the F-5A Freedom Fighter, to which the T-38 bears a strong physical similarity. Three YT-38 prototypes were ordered as part of a provisional contract awarded to Northrop in 1956. After three years of development, flight trials were undertaken to assess the performance of different powerplants, before service began with the USAF in March 1961. The aircraft has proved highly successful in service, with 1139 completed. Approximately 700 are still in service. Portugal and Turkey also use the aircraft and are likely to continue doing so for some years.

SPECIFICATIONS

COUNTRY OF ORIGIN: United States
TYPE: two-seat supersonic basic trainer
POWERPLANT: two 1746kg (3850lb) General Electric J85-GE-5 turbojets
PERFORMANCE: maximum speed at 10,975m (36,000ft) 1381km/h (858mph); service ceiling 16,340m (53,600ft); range with internal fuel 1759km (1093 miles)
WEIGHT LOADED: empty 3254kg (7174lb); maximum take-off 5361kg (11,820lb)
DIMENSIONS: wingspan 7.7m (25ft 3in); length 14.14m (46ft 5in); height 3.92m (12ft 10in); wing area 15.79m^2 (170ft^2)
ARMAMENT: none

Panavia Tornado ADV

In the late 1960s the RAF saw the need to replace its McDonnell Douglas Phantom II and BAe Lighting interceptors, and ordered the development of the Tornado ADV (Air Defence Variant) – a dedicated air-defence aircraft with all-weather capability – based on the same airframe as the GR.Mk 1 ground attack aircraft. It was realised early in the programme that to attain adequate fighter performance, it would be necessary to recess the primary armament of the aircraft – the BAe Sky Flash air-to-air missile – under the fuselage centreline. Full development was authorised in March 1976, and the aircraft shares 80 per cent commonality with its predecessor. Structural changes include a lengthened nose for the Foxhunter radar, and a slight increase in the fuselage length. Deliveries of 18 F.Mk 2s to the RAF were followed by 155 F.Mk 3 aircraft with Mk 104 engines.

SPECIFICATIONS

COUNTRY OF ORIGIN: Germany, Italy and United Kingdom
TYPE: all-weather air defence aircraft
POWERPLANT: two 7493kg (16,520lb) Turbo-Union RB.199-34R Mk 104 turbofans
PERFORMANCE: maximum speed above 11,000m (36,090ft) 2337km/h (1452mph); operational ceiling about 21,335m (70,000ft); intercept radius more than 1853km (1150 miles)
WEIGHT LOADED: empty 14,501kg (31,970lb); maximum take-off 27,987kg (61,700lb)
DIMENSIONS: wingspan 13.91m (45ft 8in) spread and 8.6m (28ft 3in) swept; length 18.68m (61ft 3in); height 5.95m (19ft 6in); wing area 26.60m^2 (286.3ft^2)
ARMAMENT: two 27mm (1.062in) IWKA-Mauser cannon with 180 rpg, six external hardpoints with provision for up to 5806kg (12,800lb) of stores, including Sky Flash medium-range air-to-air missiles, AIM-9L Sidewinder short range air-to-air missiles and drop tanks

PZL I-22 Iryda

The PZL I-22 Iryda was designed by a team at the Istytut Lotnictwa led by Alfred Baron to replace the TS-11 Iskra as the primary jet trainer of the Polish air force. The I-22 is a far more versatile aircraft, with the capability for advanced pilot training in roles such as ground attack, air combat and reconnaissance. The aircraft has a useful weapons load and can also undertake light attack missions. The aircraft is similar in both configuration and appearance to the Dassault/Dornier Alpha Jet, and has broadly similar performance. Pictured is one of the prototype aircraft; production deliveries to the Polish air force began in 1993, although with the dominance of the Aero L-29 in the inventories of former Eastern Bloc nations it is unlikely to enjoy major export success. The aircraft pictured is the first of the two prototypes, and first flew in March 1985.

SPECIFICATIONS

COUNTRY OF ORIGIN: Poland
TYPE: two-seat multi-role trainer and light close-support aircraft
POWERPLANT: two 1100kg (2425lb) PZL-Rzeszow SO-3W22 turbojets
PERFORMANCE: maximum speed at 5000m (16,405ft) 840km/h (522mph); service ceiling 11,000m (36,090ft); range with maximum warload 420km (261 miles)
WEIGHT LOADED: empty 4700kg (10,361lb); maximum take-off 6900kg (15,211lb)
DIMENSIONS: wingspan 9.6m (31ft 6in); length 13.22m (43ft 5in); height 4.3m (14ft 1in); wing area 19.92m^2 (214.42ft^2)
ARMAMENT: one 23mm (0.91in) GSh-23L cannon with 200 rds, four external hardpoints with provision for 1200kg (2645lb) of stores, including bombs, rocket launcher pods and drop tanks

PZL Mielec TS-11 Iskra-bis B

The Polish-designed TS-11 Iskra (spark) two-seat trainer was selected by the Polish air force for production in 1961, despite having lost a Soviet air force competition for such an aircraft to the Aero L-29. The aircraft became operational in 1964; improvements were made to the basic powerplant and production of the two-seat version continued until mid-1979. A single-seat reconnaissance version was also produced before this time. Production resumed in 1982 of an improved combat/reconnaissance version, and ceased in the late 1980s, with more than 600 aircraft completed. The aircraft was also produced for the Indian air force who took delivery of 50. The aircraft has now been almost completely replaced in Polish service by the I-22 Iryda, and it is likely that the IAF will replace their aircraft in the near future.

SPECIFICATIONS

COUNTRY OF ORIGIN: Poland
TYPE: two-seat combat/reconnaissance trainer
POWERPLANT: one 1100kg (2425lb) IL SO-3W turbojet
PERFORMANCE: maximum speed at 5000m (16,405ft) 770km/h (478mph); service ceiling 11,000m (36,090ft); range on internal fuel 1260km (783 miles)
WEIGHT LOADED: empty 2560kg (5644lb); maximum take-off 3840kg (8466lb)
DIMENSIONS: wingspan 10.06m (33ft); length 11.15m (36ft 7in); height 3.5m (11ft 6in); wing area 17.50m^2 (188.37ft^2)
ARMAMENT: one 23mm (0.91in) cannon, four external hardpoints for a variety of weapons up to a total of 400kg (882lb)

Republic F-84F Thunderstreak

In 1944 Republic began development of the Thunderjet, an aircraft which they conceived as a replacement for the piston-engined P-47 Thunderbolt. The first of three prototype aircraft was flown at the Muroc Dry Lake test centre on 28 February 1946. The first production aircraft were designated F-84B and entered full-scale production for the USAF in May 1947. Total production was 224. Introduction of a swept wing began with the F-84F variant, which first flew in June 1950, although problems with the Allison powerplant delayed development and service deliveries. Some 2713 F-84Fs were completed, of which 1301 were supplied to NATO forces. The aircraft continued in service with Air National Guard units until 1971. The aircraft pictured served with the Belgian air force during the 1960s.

SPECIFICATIONS

COUNTRY OF ORIGIN: United States
TYPE: single-seat fighter-bomber
POWERPLANT: one 3278kg (7220lb) Wright J65-W-3 turbojet
PERFORMANCE: maximum speed 1118km/h (695mph); service ceiling 14,020kg (46,000ft); combat radius with drop tanks 1304km (810 miles)
WEIGHT LOADED: empty 6273kg (13,830lb); maximum take-off 12,701kg (28,000lb)
DIMENSIONS: wingspan 10.24m (33ft 7in); length 13.23m (43ft 5in); height 4.39m (14ft 5in); wing area 30.19m^2 (325ft^2)
ARMAMENT: six 12.7mm (0.5in) Browning M3 machine guns, external hardpoints with provision for up to 2722kg (6000lb) of stores

Republic F-84G Thunderjet

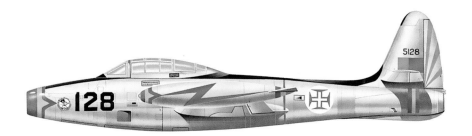

Last of the 'straight-wing' F-84 family, and the most numerous production version, was the F-84G, of which 3025 were built. This was the first single-seat US fighter aircraft capable of delivering nuclear weapons. The aircraft had provision for inflight refuelling and was equipped with an autopilot. In September 1954, using its refuelling capability, the F-84G became the first turbojet powered single-seat fighter to record a non-stop crossing of the Atlantic. Strategic Air Command retired its F-84Gs by 1956, although Tactical Air Command retained its aircraft for some time afterward. Of the total built, 1936 were supplied to NATO air forces. Take-off with full weapons load was very long and often marginal, but the aircraft provided an effective foil to the Eastern Bloc in central Europe.

SPECIFICATIONS

COUNTRY OF ORIGIN: United States
TYPE: single-seat fighter-bomber
POWERPLANT: one 2542kg (5600lb) Wright J65-A-29 turbojet
PERFORMANCE: maximum speed 973km/h (605mph) at 1220m (4000ft); service ceiling 12,353m (40,500ft); combat radius with drop tanks 1609km (1000 miles)
WEIGHT LOADED: empty 5203kg (11,460lb); maximum take-off 12,701kg (28,000lb)
DIMENSIONS: wingspan 11.05m (36ft 4in); length 11.71m (38ft 5in); height 3.9m (12ft 10in); wing area 24.18m² (260ft²)
ARMAMENT: six 12.7mm (0.5in) Browning M3 machine-guns, external hardpoints with provision for up to 1814kg (4000lb) of stores including rockets and bombs

Republic RF-84F Thunderflash

The final major production version of the swept-wing F-84 family was the RF-84F reconnaissance aircraft, with wing root air intakes and cameras in the nose. The prototype was designated YRF-84F and first flew in 1952. Deliveries to Strategic Air Command and Tactical Air Command reconnaissance units began in March 1954, and by the time the deliveries ended in 1958, production had reached 715, including 386 bought by the Air Force Mutual Defense programme and destined for users abroad. Some 25 aircraft were later modified for the FICON (Fighter Conveyor) project with a retractable hook in the nose, to provide long-range reconnaissance capability. The carrier aircraft was a modified Convair B-36 bomber. After hooking on to their long-range transport, the aircraft (designated RF-84K) were carried to the reconnaissance area. Mission complete, they hooked up again for return to base.

SPECIFICATIONS

COUNTRY OF ORIGIN: United States
TYPE: single-seat photo-reconnaissance aircraft
POWERPLANT: one 3541kg (7800lb) Wright J65-W-7 turbojet
PERFORMANCE: maximum speed 1118km/h (695mph); service ceiling 14,020kg (46,000ft); combat radius with drop tanks 1304km (810 miles)
WEIGHT LOADED: empty 6273kg (13,830lb); maximum take-off 12,701kg (28,000lb)
DIMENSIONS: wingspan 10.24m (33ft 7in); length 13.23m (43ft 5in); height 4.39m (14ft 5in); wing area 30.19m^2 (325ft^2)
ARMAMENT: six 12.7mm (0.5in) Browning M3 machine-guns, external hardpoints with provision for up to 2722kg (6000lb) of stores

Rockwell T-2 Buckeye

The T-2 began service as the primary jet trainer of the US Navy in 1960, and after nearly 40 years is now being replaced by the T-45A Goshawk. The wing of the aircraft was derived from the FJ-1 Fury and the control system is similar to that employed on the T-28 Trojan. The first aircraft flew on 31 January 1958 and service deliveries began the following July. A total of 217 T-2As were supplied to the US Navy under the name Buckeye. A more powerful version designated T-2B was also produced. The final version was the T-2C with yet more powerful General Electric engines. Two hundred and seventy three were built, some of which were supplied to Venezuela and Greece. Pictured is one of the T-2C aircraft operated by VT-23 of Training Wing 2, US Navy. Some of the aircraft in US service have been converted for use as drone directors.

SPECIFICATIONS

COUNTRY OF ORIGIN: United States
TYPE: two-seat multi-role jet trainer
POWERPLANT: one 1338kg (2950lb) General Electric J85-GE-4 turbojets
PERFORMANCE: maximum speed at 7620m (25,000ft) 838km/h (521mph); service ceiling 13,535m (44,400ft); range 1465km (910 miles)
WEIGHT LOADED: empty 3681kg (8115lb); maximum take-off 5978kg (13,180lb)
DIMENSIONS: wingspan 11.63m (38ft 2in); length 11.79m (38ft 8in); height 4.51m (14ft 10in); wing area 23.70m^2 (255ft^2)
ARMAMENT: none

Saab 105

Saab established its reputation as a designer and manufacturer of first class jet aircraft with the Draken. The success of this aircraft encouraged the Swedish manufacturer to extend their range of aircraft by developing the privately-funded 105. This aircraft is a swept shoulder-wing monoplane with side-by-side cabin accommodation for either two or four crew. Power is provided by twin turbojets. The first prototype flew in June 1963, and after successful evaluation by the Swedish air force, orders were placed for 150 production aircraft. The type began to enter service in 1966, initially with the primary flying training school at Ljungbyhed air base. In Swedish air force use, the aircraft are designated Sk 60A; the armed close-support variant is the Sk 60B, and the photo-recce version is the Sk 60C.

SPECIFICATIONS

COUNTRY OF ORIGIN: Sweden
TYPE: training/liason aircraft with secondary attack capability
POWERPLANT: two 744kg (1640lb) Turbomeca Aubisque turbofans
PERFORMANCE: maximum speed at 6095m (20,000ft) 770km/h (480mph); service ceiling 13,500m (44,290ft); range 1400km (870 miles)
WEIGHT LOADED: empty 2510kg (5534lb); maximum take-off 4050kg (8929lb)
DIMENSIONS: wingspan 9.5m (31ft 2in); length 10.5m (34ft 5in); height 2.7m (8ft 10in); wing area 16.3m^2 (175.46ft^2)
ARMAMENT: six external hardpoints with provision for up to 700kg (1543lb) of stores, including two Saab Rb05 air-to-surface missiles, or two 30mm (1.18in) cannon pods, or 12 135mm (5.31in) rockets, or bombs, cluster bombs and rocket launcher pods

Saab J 35J Draken

The final new-build air defence version of the Draken was the J 35F, which was a development of the J 35D with more capable radar, collision course firecontrol and a Hughes infra-red sensor to allow the carriage of licence-built Hughes Falcon AAMs. During the late 1980s, the decision was taken to update 64 J 35Fs to J 35J standard in order to allow three squadrons of F10 Wing, based near Angelholm in southern Sweden, to remain operational until the mid-1990s. Improvements were made to the weapons electronics, IR sensor, radar and IFF equipment. Two additional inboard pylons were added to the strengthened wing, together with an altitude warning system. Redeliveries were completed in 1990. Pictured is one of the aircraft operated by Flygflottilz 10, with Rb24 sidewinder missiles on both inboard and outer pylons.

SPECIFICATIONS

COUNTRY OF ORIGIN: Sweden

TYPE: single-seat all-weather interceptor

POWERPLANT: one 7830kg (17,262lb) Svenska Flygmotor RM6C turbojet

PERFORMANCE: maximum speed at 11,000m (36,090ft) 2125km/h (1320mph); service ceiling 20,000m (65,000ft); range with internal fuel on hi-lo-hi mission 560km (348 miles)

WEIGHT LOADED: empty 7425kg (16,369lb); maximum take-off 16,000kg (35,274lb)

DIMENSIONS: wingspan 9.4m (30ft 10in); length 15.4m (50ft 4in); height 3.9m (12ft 9in); wing area 49.20m² (526.6ft²)

ARMAMENT: one 30mm (1.18in) Aden M/55 cannon with 90 rds, two radar-homing Rb27 and two IR-homing Rb28 Falcon air-to-air missiles, or two of four Rb24 Sidewinder AAMs, or up to 4082kg (9000lb) of bombs on attack mission

Saab J 32B Lansen

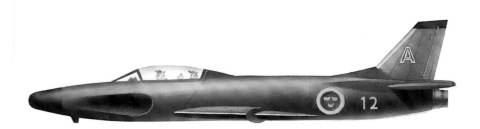

Designed to replace the Saab 18 light-bomber in service with the Swedish air force, the Type 32 was a large all-swept machine of outstanding quality, designed and developed ahead of similar aircraft elsewhere in Western Europe. Owing to its not inconsiderable size, it was capable of development for three dissimilar missions. The A 32A all-weather attack aircraft was the first into production in 1953, followed by the J 32B all-weather and night fighter, and the S 32C reconnaissance aircraft in mid-1958. The survivors of nearly 450 aircraft completed served well into the 1990s as aggressor aircraft, target tugs, and trials aircraft. The J 32B pictured here had a more powerful licence-built Rolls Royce engine than its predecessor, and S6 radar fire control for lead or pursuit interception. Between 1958 and 1970 seven squadrons were equipped with the type.

SPECIFICATIONS

COUNTRY OF ORIGIN: Sweden
TYPE: all-weather and night fighter
POWERPLANT: one 6890kg (15,190lb) Svenska Flygmotor (Rolls-Royce Avon) RM6A
PERFORMANCE: maximum speed 1114km/h (692mph); service ceiling 16,013m (52,500ft); range with external fuel 3220km (2000 miles)
WEIGHT LOADED: empty 7990kg (17,600lb); maximum loaded 13,529kg (29,800lb)
DIMENSIONS: wingspan 13m (42ft 8in); length 14.50m (47ft 7in); height 4.65m (15ft 3in); wing area 37.4m^2 (402.58ft^2)
ARMAMENT: four 30mm (1.18in) Aden M/55 cannon; four Rb324 (Sidewinder) air-to-air missiles or FFAR (Folding Fin Air-launched Rocket) pods

Saab J 35F Draken

The Draken was designed to a demanding Swedish air force specification for a single-seat interceptor which could operate from short air strips, have rapid time-to-height performance, and supersonic performance. The aircraft the Saab team, led by Erik Bratt, designed between 1949–51 is one of the most remarkable to arrive on the post-war aviation scene. The unique 'double-delta' is an ingenious method of arranging items one behind the other to give a long aircraft with small frontal area and correspondingly high aerodynamic efficiency. The aircraft was ten years in development, with the first J35A production models arriving in service in March 1960. Saab also offered the Draken for export under the designation Saab-35X, with increased fuel capacity and higher gross weight. Finland received 24 ex-Flyguapnet J34F single-seaters, one pictured here.

SPECIFICATIONS

COUNTRY OF ORIGIN: Sweden
TYPE: single-seat all-weather interceptor
POWERPLANT: one 7761kg (17,110lb) Svenska Flygmotor RM6C turbojet
PERFORMANCE: maximum speed 2125km/h (1320mph); service ceiling 20,000m (65,000ft); range with maximum fuel 3250km (2020 miles)
WEIGHT LOADED: empty 7425kg (16,369lb); maximum take-off 16,000kg (35,274lb)
DIMENSIONS: wingspan 9.4m (30ft 10in); length 15.4m (50ft 4in); height 3.9m (12ft 9in); wing area 49.20m^2 (526.6ft^2)
ARMAMENT: one 30mm (1.18in) Aden M/55 cannon with 90 rds, two radar-homing Rb27 and two IR-homing Rb28 Falcon air-to-air missiles, or two of four Rb24 Sidewinder AAMs, or up to 4082kg (8980lb) of bombs on attack mission

Saab JA37 Viggen

The interceptor version of the Viggen, and an integral part of the System 37 series, was the single-seat JA37. Externally, the aircraft closely resembles the attack AJ37, although the fin is slightly taller and the interceptor has four elevon actuators under the wing instead of three as on other versions. A considerable amount of effort was made to optimize the Pratt & Whitney-designed Volvo turbofan for high-altitude performance and high-stress combat manoeuvring, resulting in the RM8B unit fitted to the JA37. The other main area of development was the onboard avionics suite, most importantly the Ericsson UAP-1023 I/J-band long-range pulse-Doppler radar which provides target search and acquisition. Production of the JA37 totalled 149 aircraft with the last delivered in June 1990. The number 13 on the fuselage denotes Flygflottilz 13 of the Swedish air force.

SPECIFICATIONS

COUNTRY OF ORIGIN: Sweden
TYPE: single-seat all-weather interceptor aircraft with secondary attack capability
POWERPLANT: one 12,750kg (28,109lb) Volvo Flygmotor RM8B turbofan
PERFORMANCE: maximum speed at high altitude 2124km/h (1320mph); service ceiling 18,290m (60,000ft); combat radius on lo-lo-lo mission with external armament 500km (311 miles)
WEIGHT LOADED: empty 15,000kg (33,060lb); maximum take-off 20,500kg (45,194lb)
DIMENSIONS: wingspan 10.6m (34ft 9in); length 16.3m (53ft 6in); height 5.9m (19ft 4in); wing area 46m^2 (495.16ft^2)
ARMAMENT: one 30mm (1.18in) Oerlikon KCA cannon with 150 rds; six external hardpoints with provision for 6000kg (13,228lb) of stores, including two Rb71 Sky Flash and four Rb24 Sidewinder air-to-air missiles, or bombs and/or 135mm (5.3in) rocket pods

Saab JAS 39 Gripen

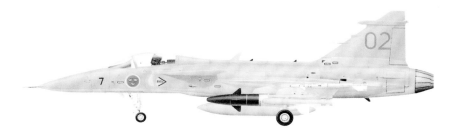

Saab has produced another excellent lightweight fighter in the form of the Gripen, and it is extremely surprising, given the outstanding performance demonstrated by the aircraft, that more export orders have not been forthcoming. The aircraft was conceived during the late 1970s as a replacement for the AJ, SH, SF and JA versions of the Saab 37 Viggen. Configuration follows Saab's tried and tested convention with an aft-mounted delta, and swept canard foreplanes. The flying surfaces are controlled via a fly-by-wire system. Advanced avionics, including pulse-Doppler search and acquisition radar, pod-mounted FLIR, head-up and -down displays (replacing normal flight instruments) and excellent ECM and navigation systems, give the aircraft multi-role all-weather capability. The JAS 39A became operational in 1995.

SPECIFICATIONS

COUNTRY OF ORIGIN: Sweden
TYPE: single-seat all-weather fighter, attack and reconnaissance aircraft
POWERPLANT: one 8210kg (18,100lb) Volvo Flygmotor RM12 turbofan
PERFORMANCE: maximum speed more than Mach 2; range on hi-lo-hi mission with external armament 3250km (2020 miles)
WEIGHT LOADED: empty 6622kg (14,600lb); maximum take-off 12,473kg (27,500lb)
DIMENSIONS: wingspan 8m (26ft 3in); length 14.1m (46ft 3in); height 4.7m (15ft 5in)
ARMAMENT: one 27mm (1.06in) Mauser BK27 cannon with 90 rounds, six external hardpoints with provision for Rb71 Sky Flash and Rb24 Sidewinder air-to-air missiles, Maverick air-to-surface missiles, Rb15F anti-ship missiles, bombs, cluster bombs, rocket-launcher pods, reconnaissance pods, drop tanks and ECM pods

Saab SF37 Viggen

The second variant in the System 37 series was the SF37, a dedicated single-seat reconnaissance version intended to replace the S 35E in service with the Swedish air force. The first prototype flew in May 1973. Production aircraft are distinguished by a chisel nose containing seven cameras, which are often supplemented by surveillance pods on the shoulder hardpoints. One forward-looking camera is used for infra-red photography; two are installed vertically for high altitude work and four are mounted in a downward facing arc for use at lowlevel. This provides horizon-to-horizon surveillance. The aircraft retain the full weapon capability of the JA37 interceptor, but the camera fit in the nose dispenses with radar of any kind. Deliveries of 26 SF37s began in April 1977.

SPECIFICATIONS

COUNTRY OF ORIGIN: Sweden

TYPE: single-seat all-weather photo-reconnaissance aircraft

POWERPLANT: one 11,800kg (26,015lb) Volvo Flygmotor RM8 turbofan

PERFORMANCE: maximum speed at high altitude 2124km/h (1320mph); service ceiling 18,290m (60,000ft); combat radius on hi-lo-hi mission with external armament 1000km (621 miles)

WEIGHT LOADED: empty 11,800kg (26,015lb); maximum take-off 17,000kg (37,479lb)

DIMENSIONS: wingspan 10.6m (34ft 9in); length 16.3m (53ft 6in); height 5.9m (19ft 4in); wing area 46m^2 (495.16ft^2)

ARMAMENT: (in secondary attack role) seven external hardpoints with provision for 6000kg (13,228lb) of stores, including 30mm (1.18in) Aden cannon pods, 135mm (5.3in) rocket pods, Sidewinder or Falcon air-to-air missiles for self defence, Maverick air-to-surface missiles, bombs, cluster bombs

Saab Sk 35C Draken

One of the two Draken variants developed for the Swedish air force was the Sk35C tandem two-seat operational conversion trainer. The other is the S 35E reconnaissance aircraft derived from the J 35D. The Sk 35C fleet mainly converted J 35As, with armament removed and without any combat capability. In 1995, only 12 remained in service with Flygflottilj, 10 at Angelholm in southern Sweden. Eleven export versions of the same aircraft, designated Sk 35XD, were delivered to Denmark, and five J 35CS (Swedish Sk 35C) went to Finland. Now virtually replaced by the Viggen, the Draken has the considerable distinction of being the first supersonic European combat aircraft. Pictured is a Swedish Sk 35C, carrying a centreline drop tank. Note the short tail configuration, adopted by the Type 55 afterburner.

SPECIFICATIONS

COUNTRY OF ORIGIN: Sweden
TYPE: two-seat operational trainer
POWERPLANT: one 6804kg (15,000lb) Svenska Flygmotor RM6B turbojet
PERFORMANCE: maximum speed 2011km/h (1,250mph); service ceiling 20,000m (65,000ft); range with maximum fuel 3250km (2020 miles)
WEIGHT LOADED: empty 7425kg (16,369lb); maximum take-off 8262kg (18,200lb)
DIMENSIONS: wingspan 9.4m (30ft 10in); length 15.4m (50ft 4in); height 3.9m (12ft 9in); wing area 49.20m^2 (526.6ft^2)
ARMAMENT: none

SOKO G-4 Super Galeb

Studies began on an improved version of the G-2A Galeb to replace this aircraft and the Lockheed T-33 in basic and advanced training units of the Yugoslav air force. Despite having a name in common with its predecessor, the G-4 is in fact a wholly new design, with a swept wing and all-swept tail, and a far more modern cockpit, housing the student and instructor in tandem seats. The rear seat is slightly raised, in a style similar to the BAe Hawk. Avionics equipment on the G-4 is far more comprehensive, with Distance Measuring Equipment, radio altimeter, radio compass, VHF radio and very high frequency Omni-directional Range/Instrument Landing System. Although the aircraft is some 25 per cent heavier than the G-2A, it can carry a greater weapons load. A small number of the large order for the Yugoslav air force had been delivered before the break-up of the country.

SPECIFICATIONS

COUNTRY OF ORIGIN: Yugoslavia

TYPE: basic trainer/light attack aircraft

POWERPLANT: one 1814kg (4000lb) Rolls-Royce Viper Mk 632 turbojet

PERFORMANCE: maximum speed at 4000m (13,125ft) 910km/h (665mph); service ceiling 12,850m (42,160ft); range with internal fuel 1900km (1180 miles)

WEIGHT LOADED: empty 3172kg (6993lb); maximum take-off 6300kg (13,889lb)

DIMENSIONS: wingspan 9.88m (32ft 5in); length 12.25m (40ft 2in); height 4.3m (14ft 1in); wing area 19.5m² (209.9ft²)

ARMAMENT: one 23mm (0.91in) GSh-23L cannon with 200 rpg; four external hardpoints with provision for 2053kg of stores, including air-to-air missiles, bombs, cluster bombs, dispenser weapons, napalm tanks, large-calibre rockets, rocket-launcher pods, drop tanks and ECM pods

State Aircraft Factory Shenyang J-6

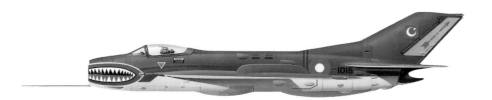

The national aircraft company at Shenyang continued to assemble a version of the Mikoyan-Gurevich MiG-19S from knock-down kits supplied by the Soviet government until 1960. In that year, however, Sino-Soviet relations cooled and locally manufactured components were used instead. The Chinese-built MiG-19S was designated J-6 and entered service from mid-1962 with the Air Force of the People's Liberation Army and became its standard day fighter. The Nanchang Aircraft Manufacturing Company in Jiangxi province were also involved in the production of the aircraft, which numbered in their thousands. Pakistan was a major export customer for the F-6, many of which remain in service in the late 1990s. These aircraft have been fitted with Western avionics, though this does not compensate for their overall obsolescence.

SPECIFICATIONS

COUNTRY OF ORIGIN: China
TYPE: single-seat day fighter
POWERPLANT: two 3250kg (7165lb) Shenyang WP-6 turbojets
PERFORMANCE: maximum speed 1540km/h (957mph); service ceiling 17,900m (58,725ft); range with internal fuel 1390km (864 miles)
WEIGHT LOADED: empty 5760kg (12,699lb); maximum take-off 10,000kg (22,046lb)
DIMENSIONS: wingspan 9.2m (30ft 2in); length 14.9m (48ft 11in); height 3.88m (12ft 9in); wing area 25m^2 (269.11ft^2)
ARMAMENT: three 30mm (1.18in) NR-30 cannon; four external hardpoints with provision for up to 500kg (1102lb) of stores, including air-to-air missiles, 250kg bombs, 55mm (2.17in) rocket-launcher pods, 212mm (8.35in) rockets or drop tanks

State Aircraft Factory Shenyang JJ-5

The physical similarity of the Shenyang JJ-5 to the MiG-15 is no coincidence. China benefited from considerable Soviet assistance when the communist government refurbished the Shenyang factory after the Second World War, and this extended to licensing machines of Soviet design to the new republic. The first turbojet-powered aircraft to be built in China were single-seat and two-seat versions of the MiG-15 'Fagot' and the MiG-17F. Chinese designers at the Chengdu factory (where the aircraft were built) developed an indigenous aircraft that incorporated features of both aircraft, and powered it with a Chinese-built copy of a Soviet engine. The aircraft flew in prototype form in May 1966 and currently serves in the air arm of the PLA as its standard advanced trainer. An export model for Pakistan, Bangladesh, Sudan and Tanzania air force is designated FT-5.

SPECIFICATIONS

COUNTRY OF ORIGIN: China
TYPE: two-seat advanced trainer
POWERPLANT: one 2700kg (5952lb) Xian WP-5D turbojet
PERFORMANCE: normal operating speed 775km/h (482mph); service ceiling 14,300m (46,915ft); range with maximum fuel 1230km (764 miles)
WEIGHT LOADED: empty 4080kg (8995lb); maximum take-off 6215kg (13,702lb)
DIMENSIONS: wingspan 9.63m (31ft 7in); length 11.5m (37ft 9in); height 3.8m (12ft 6in)
ARMAMENT: one 23mm (0.91in) Type 23-1 cannon in removable fuselage pack

Sud-Ouest Aquilon 203

Although obviously derived from the de Havilland Venom, the Sud-Est Aquilon was significantly different and in many ways more capable than the carrier-based versions in service with the Royal Navy. The French company were suitably impressed with the proposed Sea Venom Mk 52, based on the Sea Venom FAW Mk 20 to begin licensed production at Marignane, near Marseilles. This grew into an all-French family of aircraft using Westinghouse APQ-65 radar and Fiat-built de Havilland Ghost 48 engines. The single-seat Aquilon 203 had the pilot sitting slightly to starboard, a French APQ-65 radar and command-guidance Nord 5103 air-to-air missiles. Like the 202, it had full air-conditioning (a source of much contention among British pilots), Martin-Baker ejector seat and Hispano 404 cannon. Forty were completed. This aircraft is painted in the colours of Aäronavale Flottila 16F.

SPECIFICATIONS

COUNTRY OF ORIGIN: France and United Kingdom
TYPE: single-seat carrier-based fighter
POWERPLANT: one 2336kg (5150lb) de Havilland Ghost 48 turbojet
PERFORMANCE: maximum speed 1030km/h (640mph); service ceiling 14,630m (48,000ft); range with drop tanks 1730km (1075 miles)
WEIGHT LOADED: empty 4174kg (9202lb); maximum loaded 6945kg (15,310lb)
DIMENSIONS: wingspan (over tip tanks) 12.7m (41ft 8in); length 10.38m (32ft 4in); height 1.88m (6ft 2in); wing area 25.99m^2 (279.75ft^2)
ARMAMENT: four 20mm (0.79in) Hispano 404 cannon with 150 rpg, two wing pylons for Nord 5103 (AA.20) air-to-air missiles

Sud-Ouest Vautour IIN

Israel established close links with the French aviation industry soon after the Second World War. In 1957, the Israeli government struck a deal with Sud-Oeust to supply 18 Vautour IIAs, which were followed into service with the Heyl Ha'Avir by seven IINs. These aircraft played a significant role in the 1967 Six-Day War, for both bombing and interceptor missions, and acquitted themselves with some distinction. An eighth IIN was purchased in 1966. This had a lengthened nose and was equipped for electronic warfare. Israel's air force had four Vautours shot down in the 1967 war, but the remaining aircraft saw almost constant service until August 1970. The camouflage scheme on the aircraft pictured is that applied to the current generation of Israeli tactical aircraft, which is indicative of the Vautour's long-service career.

SPECIFICATIONS

COUNTRY OF ORIGIN: France
TYPE: two-seat night/all-weather fighter
POWERPLANT: two 3503kg (7716lb) SNECMA Atar 101E-3 turbojets
PERFORMANCE: maximum speed 1105km/h (687mph); service ceiling more than 15000m (49,210ft); range 4000km (2485 miles)
WEIGHT LOADED: empty 10,000kg; maximum take-off 20,700kg (45,635lb)
DIMENSIONS: wingspan 15.09m (49ft 6in); length 15.57m (51ft 1in); height 4.5m (14ft 9in)
ARMAMENT: four 30mm (1.18in) DEFA cannon with 100rpg, internal bomb bay with provision for up to 240 SNEB rockets; four underwing pylons for four MATRA 5103 (R 511) air-to-air missiles, MATRA M.116E rockets, or 24 120mm rockets, or two drop tanks

Sukhoi Su-15 'Flagon-A'

The Su-15 single-seat all-weather interceptor was developed to a requirement for a successor to the Sukhoi Su-11 (developed from the Su-7), and strongly resembles that aircraft in various aspects of its design. The most obvious similarities are the wings and tail. The initial T-5 prototype from which the Su-15 was developed was basically an enlarged version of the Su-11 with two engines, and the same pitot nose intake. The T-58 which followed had a solid radar nose housing Oriol-D radar and variable intakes on the fuselage sides. The 'Flagon A' entered IA-PVO Strany service in 1967, and some 1500 Sukhoi 15s in all versions are estimated to have been built. All these aircraft served with Soviet air arms, since the aircraft was never made available for export. The aircraft were often armed with the huge AA-3 'Anab' AAM.

SPECIFICATIONS

COUNTRY OF ORIGIN: Soviet Union
TYPE: single-seat all-weather interceptor
POWERPLANT: two 6205kg (13,668lb) Tumanskii R-11F2S-300 turbojets
PERFORMANCE: maximum speed above 11,000m (36,090ft) approximately 2230km/h (1386mph); service ceiling 20,000m (65,615ft); combat radius 725km (450 miles)
WEIGHT LOADED: empty (estimated) 11,000kg (24,250lb); maximum take-off 18,000kg (39,680lb)
DIMENSIONS: wingspan 8.61m (28ft 3in); length 21.33m (70ft); height 5.1m (16ft 9in); wing area 36m^2 (387.5ft^2)
ARMAMENT: four external pylons for two R8M medium-range air-to-air missiles ouboard and two AA-8 'Aphid' short-range AAMs inboard, plus two under-fuselage pylons for 23mm (0.91in) UPK-23 cannon pods or drop tanks

Sukhoi Su-15TM 'Flagon-F'

A number of versions of the Su-15 were produced; the definitive Su-15TM 'Flagon-F' was designed in 1971 and introduced a low-drag ogival nose radome to cover the scanner for an uprated Typhoon M search radar for limited look-down/shoot-down capability, and more powerful engines. The Su-15TM entered service in 1975. By the mid-1990s, only two PVO (Soviet home defence) units continued to operat the aircraft, and it has now been completely replaced in service by the Sukhoi Su-27 and Mikoyan-Gurevich MiG-31 from service. The aircraft achieved a degree of notoriety in 1983 when it was involved in the downing of a Korean Air Lines 747 passenger aircraft in the Sea of Japan, although it was for some time erroneously reported that this aircraft was an Su-21, in fact this aircraft never even existed.

SPECIFICATIONS

COUNTRY OF ORIGIN: Soviet Union
TYPE: single-seat all-weather interceptor
POWERPLANT: two 7200kg (15,873lb) Tumanskii R-13F2-300 turbojets
PERFORMANCE: maximum speed above 11,000m (36,090ft) approximately 2230km/h (1386mph); service ceiling 20,000m (65,615ft); combat radius 725km (450 miles)
WEIGHT LOADED: empty (estimated) 11,000kg (24,250lb); maximum take-off 18,000kg (39,680lb)
DIMENSIONS: wingspan 9.15m (29ft 6in); length 21.33m (70ft); height 5.1m (16ft 9in); wing area 36m^2 (387.5ft^2)
ARMAMENT: four external pylons for two AA-3 'Anab' medium-range air-to-air missiles ouboard and two AA-8 'Aphid' short-range AAMs inboard, plus two under-fuselage pylons for 23mm (0.91in) GSh-23L two-barrel cannon pods or drop tanks

Sukhoi Su-27UB 'Flanker-C'

Development of the Su-27 began in the mid-1970s, with the aim of producing a combat aircraft for Soviet forces comparable to the McDonnell Douglas F-15 Eagle. Given this seemingly daunting design brief, Sukhoi proceeded with impressive haste, and, by the end of May 1977, the prototype Su-27 had flown. Development from prototype stage was somewhat longer and involved some fundamental design changes, necessitated by poor structural strength, excessive drag, flutter and excess weight. It was not until 1980 that full-scale production began and service entry started in 1984. The aircraft represents a significant advance over previous generations of Soviet aircraft and presented an outstanding potential for development. Advanced avionics make it a formidable fighter. The first variant was the Su-27UB 'Flanker-C' tandem-seat trainer, which retains full combat capability.

SPECIFICATIONS

COUNTRY OF ORIGIN: Soviet Union
TYPE: tandem-seat operational conversion trainer
POWERPLANT: two 12,500kg (27,557lb) Lyul'ka AL-31F turbofans
PERFORMANCE: maximum speed at high altitude 2500km/h (1500mph); service ceiling 18,000m (59,055ft); combat radius 1500km (930 miles)
WEIGHT LOADED: maximum take-off 30,000kg (66,138lb)
DIMENSIONS: wingspan 14.70m (48ft 3in); length 21.94m (71ft 12in); height 6.36m (20ft 10in); wing area 46.5m^2 (500ft^2)
ARMAMENT: one 30mm (1.18in) GSh-3101 cannon with 149 rds; 10 external hardpoints with provision for 6000kg (13,228kg) of stores, including AA-10A ('Alamo-A'), AA-10B ('Alamo-B'), AA-10C ('Alamo-C'), AA-11 ('Archer') or AA-8 ('Aphid') air-to-air missiles

Sukhoi Su-30MKI

The SU-30MKI is a member of the Su-27 ('Flanker') series of combat aircraft. Its primary role is as an air-superiority fighter, but it can function as a strike or reconnaissance platform. Other projected roles include anti-shipping strike and a long-range air-to-air version tailored to attacking airborne early warning and fighter control aircraft from long range. The Su-30MKI was developed in conjunction with the Indian Air Force, and entered service in 2002. The first indigenously built aircraft entered Indian service in 2004. Most systems are Russian or Indian, but some French and Israeli components are also incorporated. In addition to its 30mm (1.18in) cannon the Su-30MKI can carry a range of guided and unguided weapons, including rockets, missiles and both laser guided and 'dumb' bombs. It is also capable of buddy-refuelling, enabling long missions without the need for dedicated tanker support.

SPECIFICATIONS

COUNTRY OF ORIGIN: Russia/India

TYPE: two-seat twin-engined multirole combat aircraf

POWERPLANT: two Saturn AL-37FP thrust vectoring engines delivering 83.4kN (18,749lbf) thrust per engine

PERFORMANCE: maximum speed Mach 2.35 2150km/h (1335mph) at altitude; initial climb 13,800m/min (45,275ft/min); ceiling 17,500m (57,400ft); range 3000km (1663 miles)

WEIGHT LOADED: weight: 17,700kg (39,022lbs); maximum takeoff: 38,000kg (83,775lbs)

DIMENSIONS: span 14.7m (48.2ft); length 23.34m (48ft 3in); height 6.36m (20ft 10in)

ARMAMENT: one GSh-30-1 30mm (1.18in) cannon; 8000kg (17,637lbs) of additional stores including guided and unguided bombs, missiles, rockets and external fuel tanks, plus one or two targeting or other mission pods

Sukhoi Su-35

One of the ongoing developments of the Su-27 is the single-seat Su-35 all-weather air-superiority fighter (derived from the 'Flanker-B'). This aircraft, which has similar powerplant and configuration to the Su-27, is an attempt to provide a second generation Su-27 with improved agility and operational capability. The program was severely delayed by problems with the radar and digital quadruplex fly-by-wire control systems, which replace the analogue system in the earlier aircraft. A new fire-control system was incorporated, with air-to-ground and air-to-air modes, to improve the ground attack capability of the aircraft. This is linked to a new electro-optical complex incorporating laser and TV designation for air-to-surface missiles, as well as laser ranging. Inflight refuelling equipment is also fitted. The first of six Su-27M prototypes (as it was then known) made its maiden flight in 1988.

SPECIFICATIONS

COUNTRY OF ORIGIN: Soviet Union
TYPE: single-seat all-weather air superiority fighter
POWERPLANT: two 12,500kg (27,557lb) Lyul'ka AL-31M turbofans
PERFORMANCE: maximum speed at high altitude 2500km/h (1500mph); service ceiling 18,000m (59,055ft); combat radius 1500km (930 miles)
WEIGHT LOADED: maximum take-off 30,000kg (66,138lb)
DIMENSIONS: wingspan 14.70m (48ft 3in); length 21.94m (71ft 12in); height 6.36m (20ft 10in); wing area 46.5m^2 (500ft^2)
ARMAMENT: one 30mm (1.18in) GSh-3101 cannon with 149 rounds; 10 external hardpoints with provision for 6,000kg (13,228kg) of stores, including AA-10A ('Alamo-A'), AA-10B ('Alamo-B'), AA-10C ('Alamo-C'), AA-11 ('Archer') or AA-8 ('Aphid') air-to-air missiles

Sukhoi T-50

The Sukhoi T-50, which first flew in January 2010, was conceived in the 1980s as a projected replacement for the Russian fleet of Su-27s and MiG-29s then in service. Since then the project has undergone several changes and is now a joint venture with India. The T-50 incorporates modern low-observable technologies and can 'supercruise', i.e. achieve supersonic speeds without the use of afterburners. This reduces infrared signature and greatly improves combat radius. The tail section is novel, with fully movable vertical stabilizers rather than conventional fins with rudders. It is likely that the final design will carry a cannon plus a restricted armament in internal bays, with the provision to carry additional stores externally at the price of increased detectabilty. Multi-role capability is likely, with a primary air-to-air mission supplemented with the ability to launch missiles or guided bombs in a ground-attack role.

SPECIFICATIONS

COUNTRY OF ORIGIN: Russia
TYPE: single-seat twin-engined multi-role combat aircraft
POWERPLANT: two AL-41F afterburning turbofans delivering 147kN (33,047lbf) thrust per engine
PERFORMANCE: maximum speed: 2100km/h (1304mph) at altitude; initial climb 21,000m/min (68,898ft/min); ceiling 20,000m (65,616ft); range 4000km (2484 miles)
WEIGHT LOADED: weight 18,500kg (40,786lbs); maximum takeoff 37,000kg (81,571lbs)
DIMENSIONS: span 14.2m (46ft 7in); length 22m (72ft 2in); height 6.05m (19ft 10in)
ARMAMENT: one GSh-30-1 30mm (1.18in) cannon; 2260kg (4982lb) of conformal ordnance in air-to-air mode; maximum of 7500kg (16,534lb) of external stores including guided and unguided bombs, missiles, rockets and external fuel tanks

Tupolev Tu-28P 'Fiddler-B'

One of family of supersonic aircraft produced by Tupolev with technology explored with the 'Backfin' aircraft, the Tu-22 was designed as a long-range all-weather interceptor for the Soviet air force to counter the specific threat from Western long-range missile-carrying aircraft. The two prototype aircraft were first seen publicly in 1961 with the designation Tu-102 and identified by the NATO reporting name 'Fiddler-A'. These aircraft formed the basis for the Tu-128, which entered production in the early 1960s with the designation Tu-28P. These aircraft were not revealed until the 1967 Aviation Day, after which they were allocated the NATO name 'Fiddler-B'. The crew of two are accommodated in tandem cockpits, in what is still the largest interceptor aircraft ever built. All aircraft were replaced in service by 1992.

SPECIFICATIONS

COUNTRY OF ORIGIN: Soviet Union
TYPE: long-range all-weather interceptor
POWERPLANT: two 11,200kg (24,690lb) Lyul'ka AL-21F turbojets
PERFORMANCE: maximum speed at 11,000m (36,090ft) 1850km/h (1150mph); service ceiling 20,000m (65,615ft); combat range with internal fuel 5000km (3105 miles)
WEIGHT LOADED: empty 25,000kg (55,125lb); maximum take-off 40,000kg (88,185lb)
DIMENSIONS: wingspan 18.10m (59ft 5in); length 27.20m (89ft 3in); height 7m (22ft 11in)
ARMAMENT: four wing pylons for four AA-5 'Ash' long-range air-to-air missiles

Vought F-8D Crusader

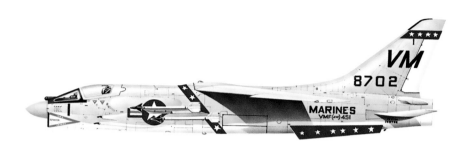

I n 1955, Vought began the development of a totally new Crusader. Designated XF8U-3 Crusader III, the three prototypes of this aircraft were powered with various J75 engines developing up to 13,064kg (28,800lb) of thrust. The aircraft were able to fly at 2543km/h (1580mph) at a height of up to 21,335m (70,000ft), but to the eternal regret of many US Navy aviators, the potentially world-beating aircraft was rejected in favour of the Phantom II. Vought continued to take the F-8 through various stages of development, hardly altering the airframe at each stage, but steadily improved the aircraft so that it remained competitive. The most potent of all these versions was the F-8D, with J57-P-20 turbojet, extra fuel in place of the underfuselage Zuni rocket pack and new radar for a specially produced radarhoming AIM-9C Sidewinder air-to-air missile. A total of 152 F-8Ds were produced.

SPECIFICATIONS

COUNTRY OF ORIGIN: United States
TYPE: single-seat carrier-based fighter
POWERPLANT: one 8165kg (18,000lb) Pratt & Whitney J57-P-20 turbojet
PERFORMANCE: maximum speed at 12,192m (40,000ft) 1975km/h (1227mph); service ceiling about 17,983m (59,000ft); combat radius at high altitude 966km (600 miles)
WEIGHT LOADED: empty 9038kg (19,925lb); maximum take-off 15,422g (34,000lb)
DIMENSIONS: wingspan 10.72m (35ft 2in); length 16.61m (54ft 6in); height 4.8m (15ft 9in);
ARMAMENT: four 20mm (0.79in) Colt Mk 12 cannon with 144 rpg, up to four Motorola AIM-9C Sidewinder air-to-air missiles; or two AGM-12A or AGM-12B Bullpup air-to-surface missiles

Vought F-8E (FN) Crusader

Despite failing to win export contracts for the F-8 Crusader from the Royal Navy, or for a two-seat version for the US Navy, Vought did manage to clinch a deal with the French Aéronavale for a version of the F-8E, even though her carrier's Foch and Clemenceau were thought to be too small for such aircraft. To create the F-8E (FN), Vought redesigned the wing and tail to provide greater lift and to improve low-speed handling. The first FN flew on 26 June 1964, and all 42 had been delivered by the following January. Nearly 25 years after entering service, Clemenceau's aircraft were involved in the Gulf War. The aircraft were slightly modified during the mid-1990s to maintain their combat-capability until the Dassault Rafale-M entered service. The aircraft pictured was operated by Flottille 12F of the Aéronavale.

SPECIFICATIONS

COUNTRY OF ORIGIN: United States
TYPE: single-seat carrier-borne interceptor and attack aircraft
POWERPLANT: one 8165kg (18,000lb) Pratt & Whitney J57-P-20A turbojet
PERFORMANCE: maximum speed at 10,975m (36,000ft) 1827km/h (1135mph); service ceiling 17,680m (58,000ft); combat radius 966km (600 miles)
WEIGHT LOADED: empty 9038kg (19,925lb); maximum take-off 15,420kg (34,000lb)
DIMENSIONS: wingspan 10.87m (35ft 8in); length 16.61m (54ft 6in); height 4.80m (15ft 9in); wing area 32.51m^2 (350ft^2)
ARMAMENT: four 20mm (0.79in) M39 cannon with 144 rpg; external pylons with provision for up to 2268kg (5000lb) of stores, including two Matra R530 air-to-air missiles or eight 127mm (5in) rockets

Vought F-8E Crusader

The final version in the highly successful Crusader family was introduced on a high when the McDonnell F-4 Phantom II was the yardstick against which all other fighter aircraft were measured. Nonetheless, Vought managed to secure a contract for 286 F-8Es, mainly due to the enhanced air combat capability that was afforded by the Magnavox APQ-94 radar (also fitted to the F-8D). Just above the enlarged radome to cover this unit was an AAS-15 heat-seeker pod slaved to the IR heads of the missiles, ensuring a high kill ratio. Fairly early in the production run, two large underwing pylons were added for air-to-surface weapons, together with guidance electronics in a shallow dorsal blister. In total, Vought delivered 1261 Crusaders, which remained in production for eight years. The final series of 48 F-8E (FN) were delivered in 1965 for use on board the carriers Foch and Clemenceau.

SPECIFICATIONS

COUNTRY OF ORIGIN: United States
TYPE: single-seat carrier-based fighter
POWERPLANT: one 8165kg (18,000lb) Pratt & Whitney J57-P-20 turbojet
PERFORMANCE: maximum speed at 12,192m (40,000ft) 1800km/h (1120mph); service ceiling about 17,983m (59,000ft); combat radius at high altitude 966km (600 miles)
WEIGHT LOADED: empty 9038kg (19,925lb); maximum take-off 15,422g (34,000lb)
DIMENSIONS: wingspan 10.72m (35ft 2in); length 16.61m (54ft 6in); height 4.8m (15ft 9in);
ARMAMENT: four 20mm (0.79in) Colt Mk 12 cannon with 144 rpg, up to four AIM-9 Sidewinder air-to-air missiles; or 12 113kg (250lb) bombs or eight 227kg (500lb) bombs; or eight Zuni rockets; or two AGM-12A or AGM-12B Bullpup air-to-surface missiles

Vought F-8H Crusader

Most F-8s underwent considerable alterations and improvement programs during their service lives. Total Crusader flight time passed 3 million hours in the late-1970s, making this one of the most cost-effective post-war fighter series. The French Navy operated the type well into the 1990s, until its much upgraded F-8E (FN) aircraft were replaced by the Dassault Rafale. From 1966 to 1970, Vought actually remanufactured no fewer than 551 Crusaders to a wide number of configurations. One of the most numerous of these 'new' aircraft was the F-8H, of which 89 were remanufactured. These were F-8D models with reinforced airframe, blown flaps, and a host of new avionics. These aircraft actually scored more air-to-air combat victories over North Vietnamese MiGs than the F-4, but achieved less fame. In 1975 the Philippines Air Force received a squadron of fully refurbished F-8Hs in 1975.

SPECIFICATIONS

COUNTRY OF ORIGIN: United States
TYPE: single-seat carrier-based fighter
POWERPLANT: one 8165kg (18,000lb) Pratt & Whitney J57-P-20 turbojet
PERFORMANCE: maximum speed at 12,192m (40,000ft) 1800km/h (1120mph); service ceiling about 17,983m (59,000ft); combat radius at high altitude 966km (600 miles)
WEIGHT LOADED: empty 9038kg (19,925lb); maximum take-off 15,422g (34,000lb)
DIMENSIONS: wingspan 10.72m (35ft 2in); length 16.61m (54ft 6in); height 4.8m (15ft 9in);
ARMAMENT: four 20mm (0.79in) Colt Mk 12 cannon with 144 rpg, up to four AIM-9 Sidewinder air-to-air missiles; or 12 113 kg (250lb) bombs or eight 227kg (500lb bombs); or two AGM-12A or AGM-12B Bullpup air-to-surface missiles

Yakovlev Yak-26 'Mandrake'

Few details of this secretive aircraft – the Soviet equivalent of the Lockheed U-2 – have emerged despite the end of Cold War hostilities. Stemming directly from the Yak-25R reconnaissance aircraft, the two aircraft share a similar fuselage and radome. The tandem seat cockpit on the Yak-25 'Flashlight' was reconfigured to a single-seat and the 'Mandrake' has a completely new long, unswept wing that was obviously designed for high-altitude operations. Bicycle type undercarriage is employed with twin outriggers mounted in wing-tip pods. Service entry was around 1957, and the aircraft was involved in operations over Eastern Asia, the Middle East and along the borders of communist territory before being retired in the early 1970s. Its replacement was the MiG-25 'Foxbat'. The aircraft pictured is preserved at the Monino Museum outside Moscow.

SPECIFICATIONS

COUNTRY OF ORIGIN: Soviet Union
TYPE: single-seat high-altitude reconnaissance aircraft
POWERPLANT: two 2803kg (6173lb) Tumanskii RD-9 turbojets
PERFORMANCE: maximum speed at altitude 755km/h (470mph); service ceiling about 19,000m (62,000ft); range 4000km (2500 miles)
WEIGHT LOADED: empty 8165kg (18,000lb); maximum take-off 13,600kg (30,000lb)
DIMENSIONS: wingspan 22m (72ft 2in); length 15.5m (50ft 10in); height 4m (13ft 2in)
ARMAMENT: none

Yakovlev Yak-28P 'Firebar'

The Yak-28P two-seat all-weather interceptor has a generally similar configuration to the earlier Yak-25/26 family, but has a high shoulder-set wing with the leading edge extended further forward, a taller fin and rudder, revised powerplant in different underwing nacelles and different nosecone. The Yak-28 was designed in the late 1950s as a multi-role aircraft and was produced in tactical attack ('Brewer-A, -B and -C), reconnaissance (Yak-28R 'Brewer-D'), electronic counter-measures (Yak-28E 'Brewer-E'), and trainer versions (Yak-28U 'Maestro'), alongside the Yak-28P 'Firebar'. The suffix 'P' indicates that the design was adapted to the interceptor role, rather than designed only for it from the outset. After introduction of the type in 1962, approximately 60 remained in service in 1990 and all have now been withdrawn.

SPECIFICATIONS

COUNTRY OF ORIGIN: Soviet Union
TYPE: two-seat all-weather interceptor
POWERPLANT: two 6206kg (13,669lb) Tumanskii R-11 turbojets
PERFORMANCE: maximum speed 1180km/h (733mph); service ceiling 16,000m (52,495ft); maximum combat radius 925km (575 miles)
WEIGHT LOADED: maximum take-off 19,000kg (41,890lb)
DIMENSIONS: wingspan 12.95m (42ft 6in); length (long-nose late production) 23m (75ft 6in); height 3.95m (12ft 11in); wing area 37.6m^2 (404.74ft^2)
ARMAMENT: four underwing pylons for two AA-2 'Atoll', AA-2-2 ('Advanced Atoll') or AA-3 ('Anab') air-to-air missiles

Vehicle name

A
Aeritalia G91T/1 24
Aeritalia G91T/3 25
Aermacchi M-346 26
Aermacchi M.B.326B 27
Aero L-29 Delfin 28
Aero L-39C Albatros 29
Aérosp. (Fouga) CM.170 Magister 30
AIDC Ching-Kuo IDF 31
Atlas Cheetah 32
Avro Canada CF-105 Arrow 33

B
BAC (EE) Lightning F.Mk 1A 34
BAC (EE) Lightning F.Mk 6 35
BAe (HS) Hawk T.Mk 1 36
BAe (HS) Hawk T.Mk 1A 37
BAe Sea Harrier FRS.Mk 1 38
BAe Sea Harrier FRS.Mk 2 39
BAe/M. Douglas T-45A Goshawk 41
Bell P-59A Airacomet 41
Boeing F/A-18E/F Super Hornet 42

C
Canadair CF-5 Freedom Fighter 43
Canadair CL-41G-5 Tebuan 44
Canadair Sabre Mk 4 45
Canadair Sabre Mk 6 46
CASA C-101EB-01 Aviojet 47
Chance Vought F7U-1 Cutlass 48
Convair F-102 Delta Dagger 49
Convair F-106 Delta Dart 50

D
Dassault M.D. 450 Ouragan 51
Dassault Mirage 2000B 52
Dassault Mirage 2000C 53
Dassault Mirage 2000H 54
Dassault Mirage F1CK 55
Dassault Mirage F1EQ5 56
Dassault Mirage IIIEA 57
Dassault Mystère IIC 58
Dassault Mystère IVA 59
Dassault Rafale M 60
Dassault Super Mystère B2 61
Dassault/Dornier Alha Jet E 62
De Havilland Sea Vixen FAW Mk 2 63
De Havilland Vampire FB.Mk 6 64
De Havilland Vampire NF.Mk 10 65
De Havilland Vampire T.Mk 11 66
De Havilland Venom NF.Mk 2A 67
Douglas F4D-1 Skyray 68

E
Eurofighter EF-2000 Typhoon 69
Embraer Tucano 70-1

F
FMA IA 27 Pulqui 72
FMA IA 63 Pampa 73
Fuji T-1A 74

G
General Dynamics F-16A 75

General Dynamics F-16B 76
Gloster Meteor F.Mk 8 77
Gloster Meteor NF.Mk 11 78
Gloster Meteor PR.Mk 10 79
Grumman F-14A Tomcat 80
Grumman F-14D Tomcat 81

H
Hawker Hunter F.Mk 1 82
Hawker Hunter T.Mk 8M 83
Hawker Sea Hawk FGA.Mk 6 84
Hawker Sea Hawk Mk 50 85
Hawker Siddeley Gnat T.Mk 1 86
Hunting (Percival) P.84 Jet Provost 87

I
IAI Kfir C1 88
IAI Kfir C2 89

L
Lockheed F-94A Starfire 90
Lockheed F-104G Starfighter 91
Lockheed F-117 Night Hawk 92
Lockheed P-80A Shooting Star 93
Lockheed T-1A SeaStar 94
Lockheed T-33A 95
Lockheed/Boeing F-22 Raptor 96
Lockheed Martin F-35A Lightning II 97

M
McDonnell F-101B Voodoo 98
McDonnell F2H-2 Banshee 99
McDonnell F3H-2 Demon 100
McDonnell FH-1 Phantom 101
McDonnell Douglas CF-18A Hornet 102
McDonnell Douglas F-4C Phantom II 103
McDonnell Douglas F-4D Phantom II 104
McDonnell Douglas F-4E Phantom II 105
McDonnell Douglas F-4EJ Phantom II 106
McDonnell Douglas F-4F Phantom II 107
McDonnell Douglas F-4S Phantom II
McDonnell Douglas F-15A Eagle 109
McDonnell Douglas F-15DJ Eagle 110
McDonnell Douglas F-15J Eagle 111
McDonnell Douglas F/A-18A Hornet 112
MD Phantom FG.Mk 1 113
MD RF-4C Phantom II 114
McDonnell Douglas TA-4J Skyhawk 115
Mikoyan-Gurevich MiG-15 'Fagot' 116
Mikoyan-Gurevich MiG-17F 117
Mikoyan-Gurevich MiG-19M 118
Mikoyan-Gurevich MiG-21bis 119
Mikoyan-Gurevich MiG-21U 120
Mikoyan-Gurevich MiG23M 121
Mikoyan-Gurevich MiG-23MF 122
Mikoyan-Gurevich MiG-23UB 123
Mikoyan-Gurevich MiG-25P 124
Mikoyan-Gurevich MiG-29 125
Mikoyan-Gurevich MiG-29M 126
Mikoyan-Gurevich MiG-31 127
Mikoyan-Gurevich MiG-35 128
Mitsubishi T-2 129
Morane-Saulnier MS.760 Paris 130

N
North American F-86D Sabre 131
North American F-86F Sabre 132
North American F-100D Super Sabre 133
North American FJ-1 Fury 134
North American FJ-3M Fury 135
Northrop CF-5A 136
Northrop F-5A Freedom Fighter 137
Northrop F-5E Tiger II 138
Northrop RF-5E TigerEye 139
Northrop T-38A Talon 140

P
Panavia Tornado ADV 141
PZL I-22 Iryda 142
PZL Mielec TS-11 Iskra-bis B 143

R
Republic F-84F Thunderstreak 144
Republic F-84G Thunderjet 145
Republic RF-84F Thunderflash 146
Rockwell T-2 Buckeye 147

S
Saab 105 148
Saab J 35J Draken 149
Saab J32B Lansen 150
Saab J35F Draken 151
Saab JA37 Viggen 152
Saab JAS 39 Gripen 153
Saab SF37 Viggen 154
Saab Sk 35C Draken 155
SOKO G-4 Super Galeb 156
State Aircraft Factory Shenyang J-6 157
State Aircraft Factory Shenyang JJ-5 158
Sud-Ouest Aquilon 203 159
Sud-Ouest Vautour IIN 160
Sukhoi Su-15 'Flagon-A' 161
Sukhoi Su-15TM 'Flagon-F' 162
Sukhoi Su-27UB 'Flanker-C' 163
Sukhoi Su-30MKI 164
Sukhoi Su-35 165
Sukhoi T-50 166

T
Tupolev Tu-28P 'Fiddler-B' 167

V
Vought F-8D Crusader 168
Vought F-8E (FN) Crusader 169
Vought F-8E Crusader 170
Vought-F-8H Crusader 171

Y
Yakovlev Yak-26 'Mandrake' 172
Yakovlev Yak-28P 'Firebar' 173